Bondi Badlands

In a career spanning more than 20 years, Greg Callaghan has written for most of the major newspapers and magazines in Australia. He is currently a senior editor on *The Weekend Australian Magazine*, and writes for *The Australian* newspaper. Greg has taught feature and news writing at the tertiary level, has an MA in Media, and is the co-author of *Men: Inside Out*.

Bondi Badlands

The definitive story of Sydney's gay hate murders

Greg Callaghan

First published in 2007

Copyright © Greg Callaghan 2007

All rights reserved. No part of this book may be reproduced or transmitted in any form or by any means, electronic or mechanical, including photocopying, recording or by any information storage and retrieval system, without prior permission in writing from the publisher. The *Australian Copyright Act 1968* (the Act) allows a maximum of one chapter or 10 per cent of this book, whichever is the greater, to be photocopied by any educational institution for its educational purposes provided that the educational institution (or body that administers it) has given a remuneration notice to Copyright Agency Limited (CAL) under the Act.

Allen & Unwin
83 Alexander Street
Crows Nest NSW 2065
Australia
Phone: (61 2) 8425 0100
Fax: (61 2) 9906 2218
Email: info@allenandunwin.com
Web: www.allenandunwin.com

National Library of Australia
Cataloguing-in-Publication entry:

Callaghan, Greg.
  Bondi badlands.

  ISBN 978 1 74114 619 6 (pbk.).

  Gay men - Crimes against - New South Wales - Sydney. 2. Homicide - New South Wales - Sydney. 3. Homophobia - New South Wales - Sydney. 4. Sydney (N.S.W.) - Social conditions. I. Title.

306.7662099441

Set in 11/14 pt Sabon by Midland Typesetters, Australia.
Printed in Australia by McPherson's Printing Group
Map by Meaghan Quirk
Cover photos from author's collection

10 9 8 7 6 5 4 3 2 1

CONTENTS

Acknowledgments ix
Introduction: A deadly playground 1

1 A newsreader vanishes 11
2 Death of a barman 34
3 A detective calls 51
4 Murder on the cliff tops 68
5 Body of evidence 84
6 Dead men walking 104
7 Case of the missing hair 128
8 The man who got away 151
9 Into thin air 173
10 A city's shame 189
11 Suspicious minds 210
12 End game 232

Epilogue: Towards the root of the evil 245

This book is dedicated to the families and friends of John Russell and Ross Warren, and the loving long-term partner of Gilles Mattaini, Jacques Musy.

ACKNOWLEDGMENTS

This book would not have been possible without the endless patience and cooperation of former Detective Sergeant Stephen Page. The details required to cover his groundbreaking investigation in all its many facets, and to recreate scenes and events, required that a thousand and one queries be answered over the three-year journey of writing this book. Nearly 40 people were also interviewed at length, too many to list. But I would like to give special thanks to Ted and Peter Russell, Craig Ellis and Jacques Musy for their kindness and time. It is a measure of the men who lost their lives at the Bondi cliff tops that they have such loving and loyal family and friends.

*The mind of a bigot is like the pupil of an eye;
the more light you pour on it, the more it will contract.*
                                            Oliver Wendell Holmes

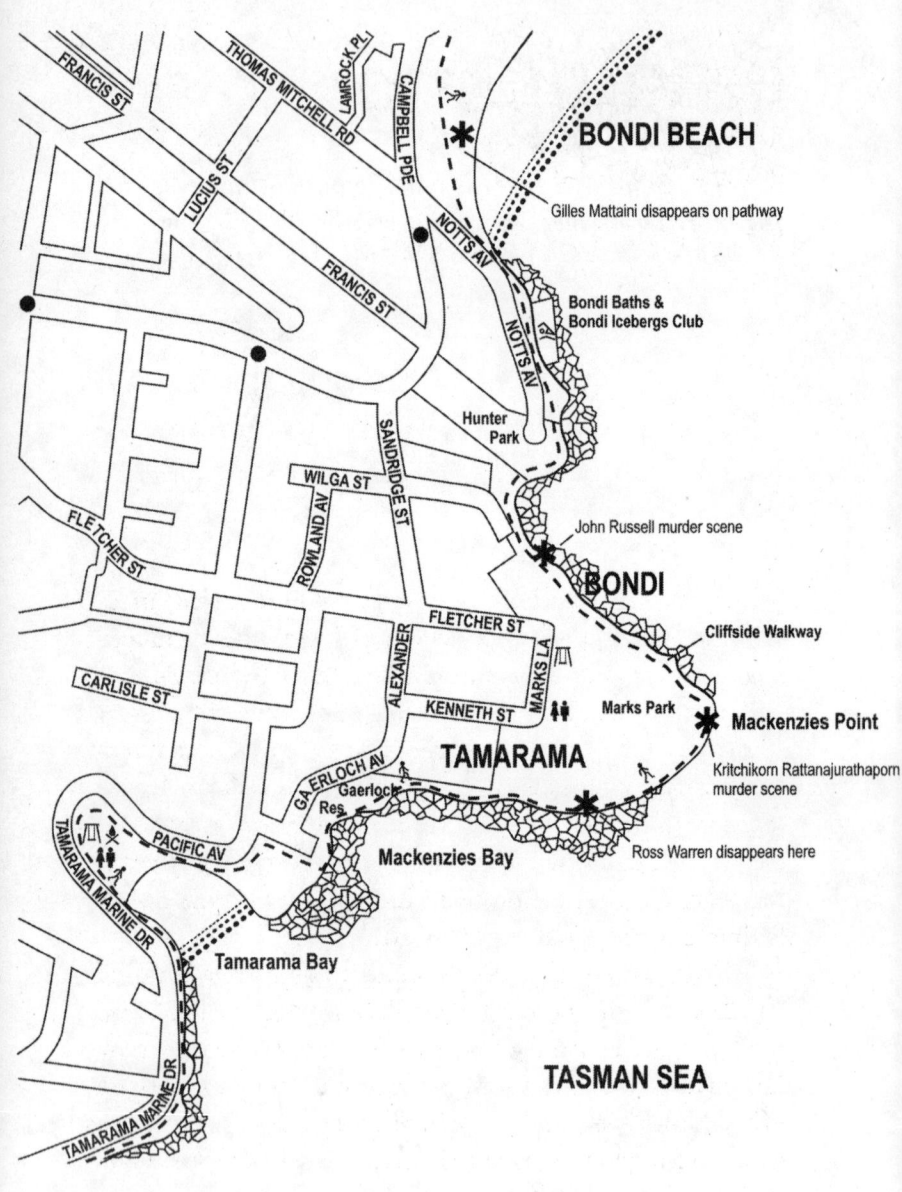

INTRODUCTION: A DEADLY PLAYGROUND

In the thick golden light of a setting summer sun, or in the shrouding mist of a winter's dawn, the headland between Bondi and Tamarama beaches in Sydney's east never looks more wild or beautiful. Come here on a sunny weekend afternoon and you'll find the concrete pathway that skirts its jagged cliff face jam-packed with joggers, Japanese tourists, smartly dressed locals and even the odd sportsman or television celebrity gaping at the stunning views. Not by accident has it become one of Sydney's most popular tourist attractions.

This is where that hardy band of winter swimming enthusiasts, 'the Bondi Icebergs', toss blocks of ice into their sea-water pool every winter, it's where the now famous outdoor art show, Sculpture by the Sea, sets up every November, and it's where rock legend Elton John came to film one of his videos in the mid 1980s, his white grand piano perched on the rocky outcrop and lookout known as Mackenzies Point. For countless thousands of years prior to the arrival of the white man, the local Bidjigal tribe carved stone implements from the boulders lining the cliff base, used the hefty sandstone overhangs as shelter from the sun and rain, and made engravings in the softer honeycombed caverns. The name Bondi itself harks back to its Aboriginal past, meaning 'the sound of water crashing on the rocks'.

The sensuous, sandy curves of Bondi Beach make it one of the most famous beaches in the world, a national icon that draws eight million visitors a year. This is where the City to Surf fun run winds up every August; it's where Max Dupain took his 'Sunbaker' photograph in 1937; it's where the last tram from the city rattled down Bondi Road in February 1960. From when the first white men knocked up lean-tos on its sandy shores in the mid nineteenth century until the early 1990s, Bondi remained stubbornly, scruffily working class, drawing artists and bohemians in the 1920s and 30s, surfers in the 50s and 60s, and the first big wave of backpackers in the 70s. Until the early 1990s, most residents paid rents in decaying Art Deco flats called the Cairo Mansions or the Venice Flats. Since then the suburb has gentrified at breakneck speed, with ritzy outdoor cafes springing up along the beachside Campbell Parade, and modest two-bedroom apartments above them fetching a million dollars or more. In the spring of 2006, a record $9 million was set for a triplex penthouse on Notts Avenue, on the Bondi side of the headland. In fifteen short years, Bondi has become one of the slickest, wealthiest suburbs in Sydney.

What still tends to smudge this shiny new image of affluence are the young overseas backpackers who continue to cram into the fast-dwindling supply of budget accommodation, and the day-trippers who pour into the suburb on weekends. You'll see them milling outside the backpacker's hotel on Campbell Parade, lounging on the beach or taking the cliff-side walk to Tamarama, or further on to Bronte, where the pathway abruptly ends. At Tamarama—or Glamorama as it's been nicknamed—you'll be face to face with the look-at-me brigade, or eye candy, depending on your point of view. Gorgeous bikini-clad sirens. Muscle-bound Adonises in Speedos. Catwalk models. Actors you recognise from *somewhere*. Step onto Tamarama Beach during Gay and Lesbian Mardi Gras time in early March and you'll be confronted with an army of gay men putting the finishing touches to their tans.

As twilight descends on the headland, however, it takes on an entirely different mood altogether, one that is all shadows and theatre. A steel railing, added by Waverley Council less than twelve years ago to the most precipitous sections of the pathway, is the only barrier between you and the treacherous rocks and churning waters below. Walk up a steep flight of sandstone stairs and you'll reach Marks Park, a grassy reserve ringed by trees, shrubs and hedgerows, sprinkled with the day's litter, overshadowed on one side by towering apartment blocks. Even to this day, Marks Park is poorly lit at night.

It was because of its special geographical features—an isolated spot in a densely populated area, and one offering shields of shrubs and trees along the way—that this cliff-top walkway and park was a popular homosexual 'beat' for decades. At a time when gay bars or venues were few, or too risky to visit, and when most gay or bisexual men married out of social pressure, closeted gay men would come to beats such as this—and Marks Park was among Sydney's most famous—to meet others, soak up the seaside view, and, if the conditions were right, engage in casual, anonymous sex out of view or go back to one of their homes if it were available.

Homosexuals. Family men with secrets. Young gay men trying clandestinely to work out whether they were or weren't. Heterosexual men who would never identify as being gay or bisexual but who occasionally had sex with men. Some attracted to the social aspects of mixing with like-minded souls; others to the sheer sexual danger. One theory has it that men prowl or 'cruise' beats because the heterosexual world has taught them to associate homosexuality with guilt, repression and disguise. Here is an after-midnight world that offers them a clandestine sexual escape—albeit a highly risky one.

The gay beat drew international headlines back in April 1998 when British singer George Michael was arrested at a toilet block in a Los Angeles park by an undercover cop, who charged him with performing a 'lewd act'. Michael, who pleaded 'no contest' to the charge, claimed he was entrapped and went on to make a satirical music video called 'Outside', which featured urinals and kissing policemen.

'Poofter bashing' at beats such as this—and they exist in public parks, public toilets and beaches—was epidemic throughout Australian cities in the 1960s and 70s. Only a small fraction of these bashings was ever reported, their victims gagged by a blistering sense of shame, and a suspicion that the police, if they weren't openly hostile, wouldn't do much about it. The stubborn, stony silence on all sides only served to fuel further violence, emboldening the perpetrators to be even more brutal and brazen.

But something different happened on the Bondi headland between 1989 and 1990. The popular trysting spot turned into a playground for killers. It was here that gay men were dragged kicking and screaming to the cliff edge, where they were hurled over in wide-eyed terror like helpless animals. The area became so notorious for screams ringing into the night and the snaking pathway so frequently bloodstained that some locals dubbed it the Bondi Badlands. From nearby apartment blocks, dim figures were often seen scurrying across Marks Park, vanishing as quickly as they came.

So no-one was too surprised when bodies started turning up at the bottom of the cliffs. These included barman John Russell, whose crumpled body was found at the foot of the cliffs on the Bondi side of the headland, his left hand clutching a clump of his murderer's hair; Wollongong television newsreader and weatherman Ross Warren, whose keys were discovered on a sea ledge, his body swept out to sea by the boiling waters below; Frenchman Gilles Mattaini who went for a cliff-side walk one Sunday evening, never to return; and a Thai national, Kritchikorn Rattanajurathaporn, who fell over the cliff edge trying to flee his attackers. Or maybe he was pushed to his death—no-one knows for certain.

Strangers to each other, these four men were linked by their similar ages, their homosexuality, and the brutal nature of their cliff-side deaths. But there were others. One man, brutally assaulted at the cliff face and nearly thrown over, was left with lifelong injuries, still petrified for years afterwards that the police wouldn't be able to protect him if he talked. And there was the bizarre case of the female impersonator who was savagely gang-raped in the bushes after being attacked and robbed.

All this violence at a time—the late 1980s—when more sympathetic treatment of homosexuality in the media seemed to be combating prejudice, when *Time* magazine devoted cover stories to the topic, when the annual Gay and Lesbian Mardi Gras had blossomed into a major tourist attraction in Sydney, drawing in excess of 400 000 spectators along Oxford Street each March. On the world stage, it was a time of earth-shaking change and liberal hope: the Communist bloc's Iron Curtain was collapsing right across Europe, culminating in the dismantling of the Berlin Wall in November 1989; the violent protests in Tiananmen Square had shaken the Chinese government; and the military juntas of Brazil, Chile and Argentina had all toppled in the previous five years. If there was a moment in time when the tolerant, democratic values of the West seemed to triumph—more than a decade before Islamic fundamentalism would test our nerve—this was it. Why then in Australia, with our sunny live-and-let-live tolerance, did such a spate of horrific anti-gay murders suddenly occur? Was this the first crack in a backlash against what some saw as a too visible, too demanding gay population?

Not really. A hatred or fear of homosexuals has always been entrenched in our culture—indeed most cultures—deriving in part from the primal need of men to prove their masculinity. The onset of the AIDS epidemic in the early 1980s—and the flush of social paranoia caused by the Grim Reaper television campaign—pushed some of this prejudice to the surface, with gays being branded AIDS carriers and spreaders. Homosexuality only became legal in NSW in 1984, and then by only a slender margin, and it took until 1997 for it to be decriminalised in Tasmania.

Even today, some in our society think that beating up gays, if not justifiable under normal circumstances, is at least understandable when it happens at an unsavoury place such as a beat. The victims have no-one to blame but themselves for taking such stupid risks. Besides, what are they thinking, having sex in a public place anyway . . . isn't it against the law?

Yes, in most states it is illegal, and yes, in anyone's language it's sleazy and distasteful. But if we were to imagine a man and woman being beaten to death because they were caught making out behind a bush in a public park, we would take a different view. What a ghastly crime, we would think. Two young people enjoying some innocent hanky-panky in public—and getting butchered for it.

That's why the murders at Bondi reflect on a dark corner of humanity and some of our deepest prejudices: an acceptance of the persecution of gays and the use of violence to confront one's own demons.

It should be stressed that the vast majority of gay men do not frequent beats; ironically, they thrive mostly in areas where homosexuality is repressed and men closeted, such as country towns and in the outer suburbs of our capital cities, where there are few if any places for gays to meet, and where men with homosexual inclinations often lead double lives.

Bizarrely, most of the deaths, disappearances and bashings at the Bondi cliff tops were dismissed by the police at the time as accidents, suicides, robberies and one-off bashings. Some of them didn't even make news stories, let alone headlines. And the investigations that immediately followed the murders were at best flawed, and at worst shambolic. Crucial evidence that could have swiftly identified the murderers of Ross Warren and John Russell was lost.

Why didn't the Bondi police at the time at least do the basics: dust for fingerprints, take photographs of the crime scene, file missing persons reports? Was it homophobia—an unstated assumption that gay men's lives aren't as valuable as others—or simple, plain ineptitude?

Here's what the lives of these murdered men amounted to in the eyes of the Bondi police in 1989. Ross Warren's disappearance? A two-page statement that wasn't even forwarded to the Missing Persons Unit. John Russell's body? A clump of hair, gripped in John's left hand with the roots still attached, carelessly lost by the police, who had his clothes washed without any forensic analysis.

Needless to say, the families of Ross Warren and John Russell were dismayed with the police response. Kay Warren could not get police to deal with her son's disappearance effectively, while John Russell's family felt somewhat abandoned without feedback as to the progress or otherwise of the police investigation. Neither family was given the impression that their loved one was important enough to warrant a proper investigation.

The cases were allowed to languish for eleven long years. It took the ferocious single-mindedness of one police officer, Detective Sergeant Stephen Page of Sydney's Paddington Police Station, to reopen the case in

2000, and slowly but surely piece together a dark mosaic of murder he codenamed Operation Taradale. It would be another five years before the families were at last given the closure they were longing for.

Back in the late 1980s, most Bondi locals considered the cliff tops a no-go zone at night because of what went on there. And even today, if you walk around the headland after sunset, armed with the knowledge of what happened here seventeen years ago, you can almost smell it.

The odour of death.

1 A NEWSREADER VANISHES

Friday 21 July, 1989

Ross Warren poked his well-coiffed head around the make-up artist's doorway, flashed his electric smile and gave her a conspiratorial wink.

'Good night, see you in three weeks!' he said brightly. 'Don't get up to anything I wouldn't do in Bali.'

Christine Jones, chief make-up artist at WIN TV studios in Wollongong, was putting the finishing touches of pancake to a late-night newsreader and looked up at the handsome face she knew so well.

'Okay, I won't,' she smiled. 'Thanks, Ross.'

Over many months of sitting in that chair, having his cheeks daubed with make-up and the bald spot in his left eyebrow, the result of a childhood scar, filled in with brown eyeliner, Ross had gradually opened up to this warm, twentysomething woman with the mop of curly brown hair and fire-engine red lipstick. 'You know about me?' he suddenly asked her one night, to which she nodded and smiled knowingly in the mirror. Their friendship now sealed, the pair wound up attending a handful of industry functions arm-in-arm. She had always loved his larrikin sense of humour, how he would give her a cheeky wink with those sexy sky-blue eyes of his if someone was being arrogant or pretentious.

Christine suddenly thought to yell out, 'You have a good weekend in Sydney,' after her friend pulled himself back through the doorway. But he was already gone and was clearly in a rush; she could hear his footsteps disappearing down the polished corridor. The newsreader was running nearly an hour late for his departure, having stayed back to have a few drinks with the production crew downstairs after reading the weekend's weather.

As Ross strode out a side exit, a clutch of dark clouds rolled in and a chill wind swept across the drab car park. His car—a chocolate-brown Nissan Pulsar—was sitting in its usual reserved spot, sporting the spanking-new rear-vision mirror he had fitted earlier in the week, which he grumbled to a colleague 'cost $38 for the mirror alone'. Ross, known for his spontaneous displays of generosity with friends and family, could also be close with a buck.

The weekend weather, so he had informed his viewers that night—Friday 21 July, 1989—would be fine, becoming a little overcast on Saturday afternoon, with the chance of a light shower or two on Sunday. The seas would be choppy on both days. He cracked a couple of jokes, in his inimitable style, but missing tonight were his trademark pastel bow tie and carnation.

Earlier in the news bulletin, after a series of South Coast stories, viewers heard that Californian Greg LeMond had won the Tour de France in the fastest time yet and Burmese pro-democracy campaigner Aung San

Suu Kyi had been placed under house arrest in Rangoon. Among the local stories was a robbery at a service station and a house fire that mercifully resulted in no loss of life.

Traffic was light, so Ross was able to make good time in the two-hour drive to Sydney. No doubt he flipped through the handful of cassettes he kept in his glove box. What album was he in the mood for tonight? Was it Rick Astley's *Whenever You Need Somebody*, Mel & Kim's *F.L.M.* or Madonna's *Like a Prayer*, three of his favourites?

Whatever was blaring out on the car stereo—he liked his music loud—you can bet his thoughts kept returning to his career. After two solid years at WIN TV—in which he had built a large and loyal fan base for his weekend news reading and lively, amusing weekday weather reports—Ross was ready for a move to Sydney. Only two weeks before, he had been in preliminary chats with network brass at Sydney's Channel 10 and had handed them a show-reel of his work.

One of the executives remarked that Ross knew how to grab an audience and that he wasn't afraid to play the larrikin to get a laugh, which was a real gift. Ross, who only months earlier had crawled onto a news desk and cuddled a teddy bear for a promotion, thought his schtick could even be a little more 'out there' for the larger, more cosmopolitan Sydney market, he put to them. But whether they gave him a gig or not, he knew time was on his side. 'The only thing holding you back,' his WIN news editor had confidently assured him, 'is your youth.'

It had been a swift rise for the 25-year-old, who grew up in upper middle-class comfort on the Gold Coast with an elder brother and sister. Adopted when he was a baby, Ross matured into an amiable, popular teenager who enjoyed playing the odd practical joke on his siblings and mates. He excelled in English and history at high school but didn't care much for sport, and by the age of fifteen was dreaming of a career in television. He scored his first break in the northern NSW town of Lismore, as a nineteen-year-old cameraman, but it wasn't long before it was patently clear that his telegenic face was better placed in front of the camera than behind it.

By the time he moved to a posting in Queensland's Mt Isa, Ross had received voice training and was doing live news-feeds back to the studio. Later, during a stint in Wagga Wagga in central NSW, he impressed many colleagues with his can-do enthusiasm, putting his hands to everything from weather reading to sports reports. In early 1987 he was offered his most prestigious role yet, at Wollongong's WIN TV as a Monday to Friday weatherman and weekend newsreader. From there he knew it would only be a short jump to Sydney.

His mentor and good friend at WIN, television producer and presenter Susie Elelman, who moved to Sydney's Channel 7 in early 1989, told him he could easily be the next Brian Henderson or Ian Ross. He had the 'it' factor, she said: a handsome face, sonorous voice and a lively personality, all tailor-made for a career in television.

If Ross could be champagne frivolous as the cameras rolled, off air he was known for his unfailing focus and workaholism. Since he started at WIN, he hadn't missed one shift, not even when he felt ill. Well liked by other members of the on-air presenting team, he made a point of winning friendships and, in the parlance of the public relations industry, had a gift for 'networking'. On Susie Elelman's last night at WIN, he made a point of coming on air with a large bunch of red roses before delivering a generous and charming speech.

After working in knockabout, working men's towns such as Mt Isa, Ross had developed a habit of keeping his private life close to his chest. It was his armour for protecting his career, he once confided to Elelman. In an image-conscious industry, he was worried he might lose his job at WIN—or worse, be forever pigeonholed—if word slipped out to the press or public that he was gay. Ross had witnessed first hand the career freefall of a WIN executive who was 'outed' by a disgruntled colleague to senior management; he wasn't keen to repeat that experience himself. 'Relax, most people here have no idea you are gay,' Elelman once reassured him.

Ross understood that in a town like Wollongong, if you were gay and wanted to get ahead, you had to keep the closet door firmly locked. He had no better example of this than the mayor himself, Frank Arkell, who maintained a charade of heterosexuality during his entire seventeen-year tenure, after being elected to office in 1975. 'I'm married to Wollongong,' Arkell evasively quipped whenever he was queried about his marital status. Although Ross didn't know Arkell personally, the mayor's closeted sexuality was well-known in local gay circles. (Two decades later, in June 1998, Arkell was gruesomely slain in his home in the beachside suburb of Albion Park by 21-year-old double murderer Mark Valera, who strangled his victim before stabbing him in the eye with his Rotary Club badge. The 67-year-old

Arkell was later named in the Wood Royal Commission for making advances to teenage boys.)

Since he had started at WIN, Ross made a habit every second weekend or so of doing the 82 km drive north up to Sydney, where he could soak up the vibrant gay scene of Oxford Street, the 'Golden Gay Mile'. Here he could enjoy a degree of anonymity, unlike Wollongong where he was usually recognised whenever he stepped out his front door. In Sydney he stayed mostly with his friend Craig Ellis, who rented a semi-detached house in Redfern with a friend called Amanda. Craig had met Ross at Easter the year before, and the pair had a fling lasting two or three months, which later matured into a strong, trusting friendship. Ross invited the 22-year-old Craig, a New Zealander, up to his family's home on the Gold Coast for Christmas 1988, and the pair spent a blissful week swimming, playing pool and watching movies.

For most of his time in Wollongong, Ross shared an old house with another gay guy and a girl. But in early 1989, having grown weary of navigating around households of flatmates, he moved into a one-bedroom ground-floor unit in an old 1940s block in Smith Street, North Wollongong. In the autumn of that year, Craig and his partner Paul drove down to Wollongong to visit their friend in his new digs, which they found dark, dingy and untidy. But interior design and tidiness had never been Ross's strong points, and by this stage he was intent on leaving Wollongong anyway.

As he had done so many times before, Ross parked his car in front of Craig's semi at 14 Albert Street, Redfern. He took the few short steps down the cement path and knocked on the door. It was around 8.30 p.m. and he still hadn't bothered to wash off his studio make-up. Craig gave him a quick peck on the cheek, passed on a phone message from a Phillip at WIN, who was also in Sydney that night, and then ordered some pizza as the three of them—his boyfriend Paul was spending the night—were famished.

The mood in the house was light, cheerful and chatty, typical for a trio of twentysomethings on a Friday night, with the whole weekend stretching out before them.

Later that evening, as they were washing up, Ross asked his hosts whether they wanted to join him for a few drinks on Oxford Street. He was in the mood for going out on the town, he told them.

'No thanks, we're having a quiet night at home,' Craig told him. Shortly afterwards Ross pulled some small pieces of paper from his jacket pocket and phoned a few mates, before returning a call to his work acquaintance Phillip, an eighteen-year-old audio operator who had started at WIN two months earlier. The pair had exchanged phone numbers several days before in the studio, after discovering they were both driving up to Sydney on the coming weekend.

'I feel like going out but no-one here is interested,' Ross told Phillip. 'Hey, do you want to meet at Gilligan's cocktail bar?'

Just before 11 p.m. Ross reappeared in the living room doorway looking devilishly handsome in his faded jeans, white turtleneck shirt and a black sports coat. He was going to have a drink with Phillip, he told them. They briefly tossed around the idea of seeing a movie the following night, discussed what was showing, and agreed on an early-evening session at a cinema in the city.

As Ross closed the door behind him, Paul's eyes momentarily settled on the scraps of paper Ross had pulled from his jacket pocket, now littering the dining table. Typical Ross, he thought. Always so messy.

He had no way of knowing this would be the last time he would see his friend alive.

◆

The Golden Gay Mile was buzzing that Friday night, springing back to life after six weeks of almost constant rain, the thumping bass of disco music blasting out of every second pub and club. At the mirror-balled Albury Hotel on the swishier Paddington end of the strip, an audience of tanned, blow-waved twentysomething men broke into peals of laughter as two blowsy drag queens exchanged campy one-liners; at the Midnight Shift, crowds of men clad in leather and denim sank beers and played pool under a thick nebula of smoke; in the Vault nightclub, groups of shirtless, sexed-up muscle men competed for attention on the dance floor.

Ross pulled into an empty car space in front of the law courts, an imposing Victorian edifice built of the same golden sandstone that once gave Sydney the moniker the 'amber city'. What luck, the newsreader must have thought: a parking spot right at the heart of the strip in Taylor Square.

Alighting from his car, he heard his name being called out. It was Phillip, grinning and waving outside the Oxford Hotel opposite. Within moments the pair were climbing the stairs to Gilligan's—an up-market, mixed cocktail bar on the hotel's second floor which boasted large bay windows overlooking the strip. It was 11.45 p.m. and there was no place left to sit. Ross bought his friend a drink, introduced him to the barman—a handsome black man with a large gold earring—and scampered off to the loo.

Ross was in high spirits, but didn't drink more than two light beers all evening, most of his bar purchases being sparkling mineral water. He half-joked to Phillip about not wanting to run into an ex of his called Ken, whom he had broken up with only three weeks before. It was a bit awkward, Ross confided, because Ken had a partner. The two WIN colleagues proceeded to exchange work gossip, swap jokes and glance admiringly at the handsome waiters in skin-tight black stonewashed jeans.

Their pub crawl next took them under the strobe lights of the Vault nightclub, in the basement of the Exchange Hotel. Here Ross ran into a few friends on the stairs, shared a few laughs, and sank another mineral water. An hour-and-a-half later and they were crossing the road to the Midnight Shift, where they had their last drinks for the night.

It was 2.15 a.m. before the pair walked back to Phillip's car. As he was jumping into the driver's seat, Phillip suggested they go to a dance party the following night at the Hordern Pavilion.

'Yeah, okay,' Ross briskly replied, perhaps imagining he would zip off to the dance party after seeing a movie with Craig and Paul.

Phillip watched Ross cross the road to his own car. But as he waited at Taylor Square for the lights to change, he noticed something odd: Ross, instead of taking a right turn and heading south towards Redfern, continued driving in a straight line east towards Bondi. Where on earth was he going, Phillip wondered. Had he missed the turn, or was he going off to some late-night tryst? Phillip, eager to get home to Glebe to grab a few hours kip before driving back to Wollongong the next morning, didn't give it much further thought.

As Ross drove the seven kilometres towards Bondi Beach in the pre-dawn darkness, a full moon was shining in the inky sky above, its light occasionally obscured by some thick grey clouds sailing over. The traffic on Bondi Road, normally gridlocked on sweltering summer days, was now a swiftly flowing stream of twinkling lights.

◆

Ross's destination—the headland at South Bondi—was enshrouded in darkness, a large swell of white water pounding against the cliff face with earth-shaking force. An icy stiff breeze was blowing off the Pacific, and the rock platform below was smothered in a film of slippery green moss, built up by several weeks of more or less constant rain.

Ross knew this terrain well; he'd been to the cliff tops many times before. In fact, his favourite romantic spot in Sydney was the lookout at Mackenzies Point, a jagged ledge of rock poking out over the Pacific midway between Bondi and Tamarama. He had come here with his former boyfriend, Greg, a part-time model and Qantas flight attendant. They would snuggle up under the sandstone overhang with a bottle of wine or a couple of beers and spend an hour or so talking while gazing out to sea. Not once during their three or four visits here did

Ross mention that the cliff tops were a gay beat. In fact, the newsreader had made a point of saying to Greg how much he detested beats.

Other close friends knew Ross better, however. It was here, above the cliff tops at Marks Park 14 months before, that Ross had met the 21-year-old Craig Ellis, who had not long arrived from Auckland. Four years earlier, in 1985, Ross had been arrested for lewd behaviour at a toilet block in Southport, Queensland, with another male in his twenties. Mercifully for Ross, who was just starting out in his career, the embarrassing incident was kept out of the newspapers, in large part thanks to the efforts of his mother.

But sexual hunger is a powerful thing, and although he avoided beats for a time, Ross was drawn back to them by the time he had moved to Wollongong. Greg knew nothing of all this; indeed, when he first met Ross at a function at Channel 7 a couple of months earlier he didn't even know the newsreader was gay. Greg was there with his girlfriend, had never had sex with another man and was completely naïve when it came to all things gay. Nonetheless, the pair immediately hit it off and exchanged numbers.

The budding friendship was cemented at a second meeting over a few glasses of wine at the Balmain dinner party of a mutual friend, Rowen Legge. The pair, the host noted at the time, spent much of the evening absorbed in one another's conversation—but the dinner party proved prophetic in a horribly different way: one of the guests failed to turn up because he had been seriously bashed in the Eastern suburbs and was in St Vincent's Hospital. 'What do we have to do to stop this?' Ross asked.

About a month later, after Greg drove down to Wollongong to watch Ross work, the relationship became sexual. In short measure Greg decided he was gay, came out to his family, and broke off the relationship with his girlfriend. It only took several weeks, however, for the self-possessed Ross to be put off by Greg's fresh-out-of-the-closet intensity. He began complaining to friends that Greg 'stifled' him, that he wasn't ready for a long-term commitment.

Shortly afterwards—in February 1989—Ross drove Greg to a quiet spot and told him it was over, only minutes after they had had sex. The pair never spoke again, only nodding at one another on the few occasions their paths crossed in nightclubs or pubs.

During the three or four times they visited the Bondi headland in the summer of 1988, Greg had never seen or encountered any trouble. He was later to tell mutual friends that he was shocked to learn it was one of Sydney's most famous beats.

◆

Ross pulled up near the corner of Kenneth Street and Marks Lane at Tamarama Beach, grabbing a spot on the ocean side of the street, now crammed with residents' cars. This was his favoured point of access to the headland; he was less likely to be seen here than at Notts Avenue, on the more popular Bondi side, where people could still be sauntering about behind the Icebreakers club in the early hours of the morning.

Ross switched off the ignition, pulled the keys out and shoved his wallet in the glove box for safe keeping. He would have no need for it where he was going, and besides, there was always the risk of robbery—after all, it contained $70 in cash, his all-important ANZ Visa card and driver's licence, as well as his Wollongong library and video store cards. Nor would he want to lose the piece of paper with the new phone number and address of an old friend from Queensland, Derrick, who had recently moved to Bondi Junction.

Ross, who had come of age during the first major wave of the AIDS crisis and the fear-invoking Grim Reaper television campaign, kept condoms in his glove box and was always scrupulous about safe sex. At beats, his sexual repertoire rarely included penetration; tonight he left the condom packet unopened.

Ross alighted from his car and checked that all the doors were locked. He shoved the thick clump of eight keys that were attached to his brass key ring deep into his jeans pocket, as was his habit.

With the minute hand on his watch now edging towards 2.45 a.m., Ross probably didn't intend to stay at the cliff tops very long. It was getting colder and windier, and a warm doona waited for him back in Redfern. He also had friends to catch up with the next day, and planned to do some shopping at David Jones in the afternoon.

Ross ambled down to Marks Park, where he stood at the top of a flight of sandstone stairs, built in the early part of the century for Tamarama bathers. The 27 sharp, steep steps took him past a toilet block on the left-hand side, and the wall of a block of blond-brick units on the right. No-one could see him from here.

Who knows what Ross was thinking as he took his first brisk steps onto the concrete pathway below, the sea churning below him, his face illuminated by the full moon above. If he was worried about the security of his car in Kenneth Street—a hot spot for car thieves—it should have been the last thing on his mind.

We'll leave what happened next—the short blast of horrifying events—to the imagination. Suffice to say that somewhere on the ocean walk that night, Ross's killer or killers were already lurking. Perhaps they were hiding behind some scrub. Or nestling in the shadows behind a rock. Or brazenly blocking the footpath. Wherever they were, they were waiting.

Waiting for the lone steps of a defenceless man.

◆

Saturday morning would have been crystal clear were it not for a few lazy, wispy clouds on the horizon. As Craig Ellis sleepily stumbled into his living room and saw that his house guest hadn't returned, he gave it little thought. He just presumed Ross had met someone in a bar and had gone back to their place for the night. Or maybe, he thought absentmindedly, he'd simply gone home with Phillip. No, Ross would never become involved with a work colleague. 'Like pissing on your own doorstep,' Ross once told him. Craig made his way to the bathroom, kicking Ross's doona slightly out of the way.

For the rest of the morning, Craig pottered about doing the usual Saturday routines of shopping, laundry and cleaning. But as the afternoon wore on, he thought it a little odd that Ross hadn't at least called. It was so out of character. The uneasiness mounted after Ross—

known for his punctuality and reliability—hadn't shown for the early-evening movie.

Something wasn't right. Craig picked up Ross's little bits of paper strewn over the dining table. There it was, Phillip's number—the guy from WIN whom Ross was to have had drinks with the night before. Two or three attempts and Craig finally got through to Phillip, who had already driven down to Wollongong and back again, at the Glebe house where he was staying with his brother.

'We drank until about two, then Ross said he was going straight back to your place,' a mystified Phillip informed Craig. 'We were supposed to be going to the Hordern tonight. When he calls, can you get him to ring me?'

Craig began phoning all their mutual friends, but the same answer—no, he's not here—kept resounding down the line.

Craig and Paul no longer felt in the mood for going to a movie. Two more hours passed before Craig called Paddington Police Station. The desk sergeant on duty told them not to worry—more often than not, young men like Ross forget to contact friends and relatives and turn up a day or two later, wondering what all the fuss is about. In any event, nothing could be done until he'd been missing for at least 24 hours.

But Craig and Paul, as much as they wanted to believe Ross was simply having a wild, sweaty time with a new lover, couldn't convince themselves.

Something was wrong. Terribly wrong.

A fitful night's sleep followed at the Paddington terrace of Paul's brother, who had gone away for the weekend and asked them to house-sit. A strange bed and the pitter-patter of rain on the iron roof added to their sense of foreboding. Craig, barely able to touch breakfast the next morning, jumped in his car and drove back to Redfern in the light drizzle, hoping against hope that his friend would be there, perhaps lounging on the couch watching television, or chatting to his flatmate Amanda.

But as he stepped into the front hallway, he could already see the empty doona sprawled across the lounge-room floor in exactly the same spot. And in the kitchen, having breakfast, Amanda relayed the unhappy news that there had been no phone messages from Ross. No word at all.

All Craig's worries would amount to nothing, of course, if his friend turned up for work later that afternoon. He knew Ross would have to be critically ill or comatose to miss reading the news, even for a single night. Ross didn't normally return to Wollongong until 3 p.m., so there was little point calling at this stage; in any case, Craig didn't want to seem alarmist to WIN staff.

But by 5 p.m. he could wait no longer. Station flacks promptly informed him Ross hadn't turned up for the scheduled 6 p.m. news bulletin and hadn't called in sick. Panicking production staff were in the throes of organising a replacement. Craig now knew with rock-like certainty that something was seriously amiss. He and Paul promptly drove to Paddington Police Station, spoke to a Constable Robinson, and filled out a missing persons report. Apart from this, the constable told them, there was little that could be done. At least for now.

Craig was grateful he had Paul with him. But what to do next? They got back in the car and checked off all the places Ross might have gone in the early hours of a

Saturday morning. 'Let's go for a drive,' Paul suggested. As if by homing instinct, they headed towards Bondi.

At first they just drove along Bondi Beach's most famous strip, Campbell Parade—on a wintry Sunday night quieter than usual—but then decided to drive around the headland to Tamarama. They cruised past the Bondi Icebergs on the Bondi side and pulled into the first available parking spot in Kenneth Street, on the Tamarama side. Darkness had now fallen, but they had no trouble recognising the car parked in front of them. A brown Nissan Pulsar. Ross's car. The car doors were locked, and all they could make out as they peered through the windscreen was a small pile of McDonald's wrappers littering the front passenger seat.

The pair immediately returned to Paddington Police Station and informed Constable Robinson of the location of Ross's car. 'Please do something,' they entreated. They were asked to wait while the two officers in charge made a series of phone calls. Before they knew it they were being chauffeured by police car to Glebe Morgue in Sydney's inner west, about six kilometres away. The body of a man about Ross's age had been found in the ocean late that afternoon, they were told. He was located just a few kilometres from Bondi at Dover Heights and his body could have been carried there by the tides, which had been unusually strong.

Craig was asked to provide a detailed description of Ross, while Paul, now visibly upset, sat next to him. The wait—which may have been no more than ten or fifteen minutes—seemed like an eternity. Although he could clearly hear the voice of the superintendent returning from the cool room, Craig was overwhelmed by a feeling of unreality.

'It's okay,' the voice said. 'Your description of Mr Warren doesn't match that of the young man here.'

Paul's first reaction was relief that it wasn't Ross. His second reaction was relief he didn't have to walk into that room with Craig and identify a dead body.

There was near-silence in the car as they were driving home, Craig's thoughts turning to the unidentified stranger lying back at the morgue. Were the friends and family of this young man at this very second frantically searching for him, just as they were for Ross? And what had happened to him? Had he drowned? Suicided? Been a victim of a random act of violence? Had he disappeared at the Bondi cliff face too? Craig's heart sank. This young man could so easily have been Ross, the friend he had been sharing laughs with only 36 hours before.

All this rumination still didn't answer the nagging question: where the hell *was* Ross? Was he hurt, lying somewhere in searing pain? As Craig slid into bed that night, his thoughts drifted to the next room, where Ross's belongings still lay. His spare jacket. Toiletries bag. Waiting for his return.

◆

Up in Queensland, Ross's mother Kay was also having a restless night, although she had no idea her son had disappeared. Ross made it a habit to call his mother every Sunday night, and she had stayed up for a call that never came. Nor had there been any answer when she called her son's Wollongong flat. Only on the following morning, Monday, did she receive a call from WIN asking if she knew where Ross might be. She immediately phoned the police, who directed her to Bondi Police Station where Detective Sergeant Kenneth Bowditch told her that Ross's car had been found. Kay, now frantic, immediately called her husband at work and booked flights to Sydney.

There was no way Craig and Paul could go about their normal business on Monday. Craig, an accountant at North Sydney, asked for the week off to look for his friend; Paul decided to skip university classes. By lunchtime, fed up with too much empty reassurance and not enough action by the police, the pair drove directly to Marks Park, bypassing the police stations in Paddington and Bondi. Ross's car was still in the same spot in Kenneth Street, and there was no evidence the police had arrived, let alone searched it.

The pair spent the next hour or so scouring Marks Park in search of something—anything—that might lead them to Ross. They even knocked on a few ground-floor doors of apartment blocks on Kenneth Street and Marks Lane to ask if anyone had seen their friend. Nothing. Craig lost count of the number of times he paced up and down the cliff walk looking for clues. Almost on the point of giving up, he noticed a rocky staircase leading down to the foreshore of Mackenzies Bay. And that's when he spotted something glinting in the morning sunshine. An object that, when he got a closer look, made the blood drain from his face.

Tucked deep in a pocket in the honeycombed rock face was a set of keys that he recognised instantly from the brass key ring.

'I've found Ross's car keys,' Craig yelled out to Paul, who was standing on the cliff top above. Paul immediately ran to a public phone box near Marks Park to call the police.

What followed seemed to be a rush of activity. Two constables conducted their own doorknock of Kenneth Street, but no-one seemed to have heard anything, let alone noticed the car, which hadn't moved in two days. They also combed for evidence in Marks Park. Craig and Paul were later assured that the Water Police and Air Wing would be called in.

By the following morning, reports of Ross's disappearance were hitting television and radio news bulletins across the country and the first newspaper stories were appearing. South Coast television viewers flooded WIN with concerned enquiries. The station's news editor, Terry Moore, told television and newspaper reporters that Ross's failure to turn up for work was totally uncharacteristic.

'In the four years he has worked here, he has never done anything like this before,' he said. 'We just can't believe it. Naturally all the staff here are very concerned about Ross.' An article in *The Daily Telegraph* claimed police believed Ross had been murdered, but it was never labelled a murder investigation. By week's end, lurid headlines were appearing in the local Wollongong paper, the *Illawarra Mercury*—exposing Ross's arrest at a Gold Coast beat—while the television news showed grabs of drag queens on Oxford Street. It would have been the last thing Ross would have wanted.

Ross's distressed parents arrived in Sydney on Wednesday morning from their Gold Coast home. After spending most of the morning at Paddington Police Station, Kay and Alan Warren drove to Wollongong, where they joined local police in searching Ross's flat.

The first thing they were looking for, of course, was a suicide note, but all they found was a very untidy unit that looked like it hadn't been lived in for several days. Scientific squad officers and detectives spent hours combing each room in an unsuccessful search for clues, taking away contact books and papers they thought might be useful for their enquiries. They also checked Ross's bank accounts to see if they'd been used. Nothing.

Later that week, Ross's parents visited Craig at his Redfern house. They had called in to pick up Ross's belongings before driving his car back to Queensland. Tears welled in Kay's eyes as they ran over the events of the past few days. As she became more and more distressed, Craig tried to turn the conversation towards happier times, to the Christmas they'd all shared together only seven months before.

After a moving farewell hug, Craig's heart sank when he saw Ross's father pull the now familiar car keys out of his pocket, and pick up the bag containing his son's belongings, now the bric-a-brac of a dead man. But the most excruciating moment of all was watching the brown Nissan disappear down the street, like a lover disappearing out of one's life forever.

If the Wollongong police seemed to be on the boil with the investigation, dusting for fingerprints and taking photographs of Ross's unit, the interest of the police back in Bondi seemed to have stalled, if indeed it had ever really kick-started. Neither Ross's car nor his set of keys was fingerprinted.

Only a few days later, without Ross's body being

found or his disappearance explained, the senior detective coordinating the investigation, Sergeant Bowditch of Bondi Police, closed the case. In his report in August 1989, Bowditch wrote:

> There is nothing to suggest that Ross Warren's disappearance was the result of foul play or a deliberate ploy on his part to disappear. He was highly regarded by his employers and amongst his friends, and our inquiries revealed that he appeared to enjoy a fruitful and happy lifestyle. Investigating police are of the opinion that the missing person has fallen into the ocean in some manner and it is anticipated that in the near future his body will surface and be recovered. I am not able to offer any explanation as to how he would have fallen into the water only that the area near where the keys were located is a treacherous rock formation which at the present time is secreting a lot of water and moisture from recent rains.

But Ross's body never did wash up. He had seemingly vanished into thin air. Over the next few months, there were alleged sightings of him in a bar in Sydney and a busy street in Adelaide, but these reports were investigated and found to be unreliable. Then there was a mystery phone call on the first anniversary of his disappearance. A switchboard operator at WIN had received a call from a man purporting to be Ross, saying he was alive and well and living in Central Australia.

'Hi this is Ross Warren, I just want to let you know that I'm alive, and to say hello to my friends at WIN TV,' the caller said.

The phone call later proved to be a hoax.

The unsolved case collected dust for more than eleven years, its file hopelessly short on the basic procedures that form any major investigation. Ross's car hadn't been dusted for fingerprints, nor were any photographs taken of it at the 'crime scene'. Although a search by the Air and Water Police is mentioned in the report, there are no records with the water or air wings to confirm these actually took place. The report was not forwarded to the Missing Persons Unit, nor was any brief of evidence submitted to the coroner. The file hadn't even been stamped 'death by misadventure', that vague, open finding that can mean accidental death or suicide.

Craig and Paul's lives went on of course after Ross's disappearance, the two spending the next twelve years together in a relationship. At the end of 1990 their careers took them to separate overseas destinations: Paul to Hong Kong and Craig to London.

Craig didn't hear anything further about Ross's fate, or for that matter about any of the other disappearances and murders that were to bloody the Bondi cliff tops over the next two years.

Paul did, however, receive one phone call while he was living in Hong Kong in mid 1990. A Detective Sergeant Steve McCann explained that a Thai man had been murdered on the Bondi headland, not far from where Ross Warren had disappeared. McCann wanted to know more about the circumstances surrounding Ross's vanishing act, but refused to elaborate what this had to do—if anything—with the murder of the Thai man.

After that single disturbing phone call, Paul never heard from the police again.

At least, not until a winter's day in the new millennium.

2 DEATH OF A BARMAN

Wednesday November 22, 1989

John Russell was leaning back against the semi-circular bar of the Bondi Hotel, schooner of VB in hand, daydreaming of his new life. In the fading light of this balmy November evening, as he gazed out through the grand French doors towards the most famous sea front in Australia, the wiry, chestnut-haired 31-year-old was filled with a wonderful sense of possibility. Fortune seemed to be smiling on him.

Only a couple of months earlier he and his younger brother Peter had each inherited nearly $100 000 from their maternal grandfather, and John intended to use the money to build a kit home on his dad's idyllic property at Wollombi, near Cessnock in NSW. He'd just selected the kit home that would be delivered in a few weeks, and he had quit his job as a maintenance worker at Rose Bay Primary School and his part-time job at the BP service station, also in Rose Bay. His bags were all piled up beside the couch in the living room of the flat he shared with Peter and his nephew.

What could be a better place for a farewell drink to Bondi—and Sydney—than the grand old lady herself, the Bondi Hotel, remarked John, fishing a cigarette from his packet of Peter Stuyvesant and turning to his old mate Dino, who was perched on a bar stool beside him.

Whenever Dino was visiting John in Bondi—he lived in a boarding house in Surry Hills, 10 minutes walk to the Golden Gay Mile—it was here that they would inevitably come, to this salmon-coloured wedding cake of a building with colossal balconies, outsized French windows and doors, and a clock tower rising in the centre, all testament to Bondi's first boom age in the 1920s, when Sydney's working classes discovered the cheap and sunny pleasures of the beach on Sunday afternoons.

John estimated that once he had forked out the final payment for the kit home, he would be left with more than $30 000, which he intended to set aside to fund another long-cherished dream: to spend a year travelling around Australia.

'Why don't you come with me?' he asked Dino, who nodded agreeably.

'Yeah, why not mate,' Dino replied.

With a few strands of his brown hair dangling over his forehead, a few days worth of growth crowding his oval face and his hand digging into a bag of potato crisps, John hadn't looked so well in ages, Dino thought.

'Another one?' asked John, pulling a note straight out of his Levi's pocket.

'Where's your wallet?' Dino asked.

'Lost it, mate,' John sighed, explaining that he probably left it in the back seat of a taxi when he was on his way back from Oxford Street the previous Friday night.

'Damn nuisance,' he added, explaining that it contained his licence and Medicare card. Luckily, he'd left his Visa card at home that night. It wasn't the first time John had lost his wallet: as far back as his teens, he had a reputation for misplacing it.

On one of the television screens behind them, the 7 p.m. ABC news was announcing that Lebanese President René Moawad had been killed in his motorcade in West Beirut, and that more than 500 000 people in Prague had assembled in peaceful protest—the so-called Velvet Revolution—against the Communist government. The Berlin Wall had already fallen to widespread euphoria less than two weeks before, and now masses of East Germans were crossing the border into West Germany. Fifty years of communism in Eastern Europe, newsreader Richard Morecroft announced, seemed to be coming to an end.

John had an important date coming up himself. The following Tuesday—November 28, 1989—he would be celebrating his 32nd birthday. Only this time, instead of the usual drinks and restaurant meal in Bondi, he told Dino, he would be raising a toast with his dad and some of the locals at the Wollombi property. He flashed an impish smile, picked up his beer and clinked glasses with his old friend.

'Here's to your new start,' Dino declared.

'I gotta say, I'm gonna really miss Bondi,' replied John.

His old mate knew he would. Bondi was in John's blood.

Like his grandfather and great grandfather before him, John and his brother Peter were born and bred here:

they grew up in one of the rambling, deep-verandahed brick-and-tile bungalows that were once the beachside suburb's trademark. The four-bedroom house at 87 Ocean Street, owned by John's maternal grandfather, was about ten minutes walk to the beach, and had been in the family for generations. The house was bought from the early profits of two cake shops—Cleck's Cakes—that John's maternal grandad ran for more than 50 years, until his retirement in the 1960s.

It was a blissful childhood for the two brothers, who walked to Bondi Public School together most mornings, occasionally getting into scuffles with other boys along the way. Young John was always quite skilled at protecting himself—quick eyes, good moves, strong arms—despite his slight, shortish frame. In high school at Waverley College he could give as much as he got—as much with his tongue as his fists if his opponent was bigger and taller.

The Russell boys loved the outdoors. Their father Ted took them abseiling off the cliffs at Nielsen Park, fishing off Watsons Bay and exploring the rivers of the Royal National Park in rubber dinghies. At least once or twice a year, Ted packed up the family car—at first a 1953 Vanguard, later trading up to a sleek Holden station wagon—and set off on extended camping trips, driving as far afield as outback Queensland, Fremantle and Darwin. One year, when John was fourteen and Peter twelve, they all climbed to the top of Ayers Rock, where John was mesmerised by the sight of two eagles nesting.

When John's mother enrolled him in judo classes when he was twelve, she wanted him to 'be prepared for the bully that may be coming'. She had no way of anticipating, of course, just how many bullies there would be.

She died of kidney problems in 1982, only a month or so before John's 25th birthday.

Not all the pursuits of the two brothers were 'boys' own' adventures, however: their parents had been award-winning ballroom dancers in their youth, so as soon as the boys were old enough they were ferried to Seagar's Dance Studio in the city for lessons. John quickly showed a greater aptitude and passion for dancing than his younger brother. Some years later he would show off some of his moves on disco dance floors, but not quite the discos his parents would have imagined, or hoped for.

John was about nineteen when Peter suspected his brother might be gay. John seemed to be mixing more and more with gay people and no longer tried to hide the fact he was going to gay bars. About a year later he got a job at a bar called Charlie Brown's in Pitt Street, which had a regular gay clientele, although it was not trading as a gay bar. As he met more and more gay people, John gradually became more comfortable about his own sexuality.

By this time—early 1978—Oxford Street, located only a few blocks away from Charlie Brown's, had emerged as a gay strip, with a cluster of new bars and clubs joining the two or three that had been there for nearly a decade. The first Mardi Gras was held in June of that year, which turned into a major demonstration after police tried to block the access route. There were over 50 arrests, outrage from civil libertarians and a blaze of nationwide publicity. Australia's gay movement was born. John had accompanied a friend that night, but made a hasty exit at the first sign of trouble, thus avoiding arrest.

For a young man like John, taking his first steps out of the closet, it was a liberating, free-spirited time. The first cases of HIV/AIDS were still two years away, and there was a shiny new optimism that things could only get better for gay men like him. He landed a part-time job at a new 'mixed' dance club on Oxford Street called Patch's, which led to a higher-paying gig as a bar manager at what was then the hippest gay club on the strip, the Tropicana.

As the evening wore on, John and Dino shared many memories of pulling beers together at the Tropicana all those years before, the bass of Sylvester's out-and-proud gay anthem 'You Make Me Feel (Mighty Real)' on the dance floor, the smoke machine going into overdrive and the occasional faint waft of amyl nitrate emanating from certain dark corners of the club. The pair had met when they were both starry-eyed nineteen-year-olds, imagined for a brief time they were in love, but soon decided they were better suited as friends. John had helped land Dino a job at the Tropicana, and the two regularly stayed back for a few drinks together after a shift.

Like all gay dance clubs of that era, the Tropicana was located behind blackened windows on the second floor. No shopfront on the street; just a discreet small sign. To get in you had to climb a steep, narrow staircase and pay $2 admission, after which you would have the choice of two bars, and a huge dance floor half encircled by a lounge area. (Today it is the site of a canyon-like two-storey gay bar and nightclub called the Midnight Shift.)

John was a popular barman, with an easygoing manner and cocky sense of humour that meant he earned plenty of tips—and usually a phone number or two by the end of each shift. Although he always seemed to have plenty of friends, John struggled to find a long-time partner, tending to have occasional relationships lasting two or three months before moving on. Whenever either of them broke up with a lover, John and Dino would commiserate with one another over a beer—or maybe four or five—about the commitment failings of men, inevitably winding up with a good old belly laugh about their own romantic shortcomings.

He may not have been a big man—at just a whisker under 170 cm one friend affectionately called him 'bite-sized'—but John was no shrinking violet. He was the first person staff turned to if a disorderly patron had to be removed from the bar, forcefully but discreetly.

As he matured into his late twenties and early thirties, John's involvement with gay community activities diminished somewhat and he slowly gravitated away from gay bar work. He got a job at the BP station at Rose Bay, and helped his brother—now a single father—raise his nine-year-old son, Alan. After their grandfather passed away in September 1989 and the family house in Ocean Street was put on the market so that the proceeds could be divided among relatives, the brothers moved into a three-bedroom flat around the corner.

Besides his two jobs, John spent up to three nights a week coaching junior rugby league and soccer at Rose Bay and Double Bay primary schools. The small family was close and happy. Peter's son Alan saw John as a second father—John was the one who made his lunches, washed his clothes and more often than not picked him up from school. Peter and his former wife had split up when Alan was just two, and shortly after he was granted full custody of his son Peter moved back into the family home in Ocean Street, and John offered to help out. For several years—until Peter met his new partner, Donna—John managed the house, bought the groceries, made sure the bills were paid on time, and kept a watchful eye on their ailing grandfather, a diabetic.

'Moving away from Alan will be the hardest thing,' John told Dino. But he was thrilled that Peter had a new woman in his life, someone who so clearly adored her new stepson.

By about 11 p.m., having shouted dinner and beers, and nearly out of cash, John decided to call it a night. The pair were to hook up again the following evening with a small clutch of close friends at the Waverley Legion's Club, to toast John's final Sydney farewell.

On Friday morning, he told Dino, his father was driving down to Sydney to pick him up and drive him back to the farm. 'And then it's goodbye to Bondi,' John said merrily, slapping his mate on the back as they walked through the doorway.

As he turned to make his way to the bus stop around the corner, Dino glanced back for a moment at his old mate ambling down Campbell Parade towards home. It crossed his mind that this would be the last time the two of them would share a beer together for quite some time.

Dino would have almost reached the bus stop by the time John crossed the road to the beach, instead of turning right towards his flat. He had decided—probably on the spur of the moment—to go to the cliff tops.

He knew it was a dangerous place at night. He knew that it was especially risky if you'd had a few drinks. A couple of his mates had wound up with black eyes and cracked ribs after going to beats. John had repeatedly said he had nothing but contempt for gay bashers, for the way they hunt in packs so they won't get hurt themselves.

'They're gutless,' he once fumed to Dino. 'They'd never take you on, one-on-one, unless they were twice your size.'

So why then, on his final night in Bondi, on the eve of making a new start in the country, did he make the fatal decision to turn right instead of left, to go to the headland instead of straight home? Maybe it was the sultry late spring evening, maybe it was his own quirky way of saying farewell to Bondi, or maybe it was just the booze reducing his inhibitions and customary commonsense, but go to the beat John certainly did.

He had no way of knowing as he headed towards the cliff tops that his would-be killers lay in wait.

◆

Only one other person remembered seeing him that night—a thirtysomething man who walked past John on the pathway at 11.45 p.m. The beat had been deathly quiet that night, and he was on his way home, earlier than usual. He gave the slim, shortish man in the torn jeans and red jersey a sidelong glance as they passed one another.

We may never know exactly what unfolded next, but we can guess that it probably wasn't very different from the treatment meted out to Ross Warren. John would have been surrounded, overpowered, bashed and finally pushed or thrown over the cliff face.

If there were no witnesses to the murder, apart from the killer or killers, at least one person probably heard it, a thirtysomething local nicknamed 'Red', who believed he was on the other side of the headland that windy night. He described a 'commotion' shortly after midnight, with voices and yells ringing out, although he couldn't distinguish what was being said.

'Red' relayed the story more than a week later to another regular at the cliff tops called Rod, who had read about the death of John Russell in the gay papers and offered to drive this potential witness to Bondi or Paddington Police Station to make a statement. 'Red', however, flatly refused, saying he didn't want any trouble. Rod only saw him once or twice more on the headland, and on those occasions he swiftly disappeared into the shadows.

Almost three months to the day after Ross Warren disappeared from the cliff tops near Mackenzies Bay, John Alan Russell also met his fate, on the opposite side of the headland.

◆

The following night Dino and six other close mates waited at the Legion's Club for nearly two hours for a friend who would never show. Typical John, they thought at first, always running late. But as the hours wore on they grew mystified that he had forgotten to turn up to his own farewell. At 11 p.m., most of them sauntered out, disappointed that they hadn't been able to say a final goodbye to their friend. A friend who, unbeknown to them, was lying in a morgue less than five kilometres away, a friend whose family the police were unable to track down immediately because of a missing wallet and driver's licence, lost only the week before.

But John Russell was at least no John Doe. In a crumpled packet of Peter Stuyvesant, tucked behind the tin foil and fourteen cigarettes, was John's National Australia Bank credit card, with his name clearly embossed on the bottom right-hand side. The killers, after pushing John over the cliff, must have tossed what they thought was a half-empty packet of cigarettes onto the rocks below. Then, no doubt disappointed with the few shekels in his pockets—and no wallet to steal—John's attackers contemptuously threw the $4.60 in stray coins over the cliff edge towards John's unconscious, but still breathing, body. It would take another 45 minutes for the deepest circuits in his brain to finally shut down.

And so, as the coroner at Glebe Morgue solemnly snapped on her latex gloves for the autopsy on John's body, the crime scene police were busy requesting his address details through the National Australia Bank. They anticipated they would be notifying the victim's family later that afternoon.

But there was a hitch. John hadn't bothered to advise the bank of his house move more than three weeks before. So it issued the Ocean Street address, where John had lived all his life, and the police turned up to a now-empty house with a FOR SALE sign.

◆

It was a clear blue Bondi morning—Thursday November 23—bright and steaming hot. Out soaking up the sunshine at the cliff tops was a local gym manager and personal trainer, killing half an hour before his next appointment. On a whim, instead of briskly walking up to Mackenzies Point as was his routine, he bounded down three wide dirt stairs on the left-hand side of the pathway, which led on to a deeper flight of stairs carved into the rock face. On the large rock platform below, he half expected to see a couple of early-morning anglers, the waves lapping at their feet. Instead, about ten metres away, he saw a bloodied body lying face down, with some coins scattered nearby, and what appeared to be a crushed packet of cigarettes.

Breathing heavily, and sensing the worst, he ran over to the body and checked for signs of life. No movement in the rib cage. No pulse. He immediately ran up to a block of units nearby which were being renovated and alerted one of the builders, who called the police on his car phone. Ambulance officers arrived within fifteen minutes, but John was immediately pronounced dead. It was 10.45 a.m. Less than an hour and a half later, John's body was lying on a cold slab at the Glebe Morgue.

◆

Back at Bondi, Peter Russell had dropped his son off to school and was getting on with his working day as an ancillary worker at Double Bay Public School. He wasn't worried that John hadn't come home the night before. John had no doubt set off for Oxford Street after sinking a few schooners with Dino; he had probably struck it lucky and would rock up at home in the afternoon, as he had done so many times before. After all, it wasn't as if he needed to be at work at nine o'clock sharp the next morning; he had already quit both jobs.

But when Peter came home from work that afternoon and found his brother still hadn't returned, he became anxious—much more so when he learned later that night that John hadn't turned up for his farewell drinks. Donna, who had only moved into the apartment some weeks before, suggested they should call the police, just to be on the safe side. But it was late and the officer at Bondi Police Station gave them the usual drill: nothing much can be done in the first 24 hours.

A restless night followed and still no word from John. Peter was at the school for only five or ten minutes the next morning when an officer from Bondi Police Station approached him in the playground. The moment Peter saw the blue uniform he knew something truly terrible had happened. 'When was the last time you saw your brother?' the constable enquired. After Peter replied the night before last, and that he had already reported him missing, the constable explained that a body had been found on a rock platform at Bondi.

'I'm sorry, sir, but would you be able to come to Glebe Morgue with us to identify if that body is your brother?'

Peter felt bewildered and in disarray as he was driven to the morgue, but when he stared down at his brother's lifeless, ashen face it was as if a part of his soul had been ripped out. There is nothing like the reality of a dead body to make it sink in that someone is gone forever. Peter wept quietly for a few minutes as he gazed down at John's battered and bruised face, and the gaping wound near his left eye.

'John and I were as close as brothers can be,' he told a detective at Bondi station afterwards, before making a statement. 'We'd grown up together; we've spent most of our lives together.'

It was barely 10 a.m. and already he'd lost his closest mate in life. If breaking the news to his son Alan was going to be wrenching—John had been like a second dad to him—he was at a loss as to how to prepare his father for the devastating news. He couldn't bring himself to tell him over the phone.

So when Ted knocked on his front door the next morning, Peter asked him to sit down and drink some water. 'Dad, I'm afraid something terrible has happened to John,' he said.

What had begun as a happy, bright spring morning for Ted—picking up his eldest son for a new life in the country—instead turned into every parent's worst nightmare. For the rest of the day, father and now his only son were caught up in the inevitable gloomy, grey haze of sorting out funeral arrangements.

John's funeral—at St Mary's in Waverley—drew more than 150 mourners, some from as far afield as Queensland and Victoria. The wake back at the house in Ocean Street, which still hadn't sold, drew a crowd as diverse as it was sombre—from family and school friends to former drag queens John had known while working at Patch's and the Tropicana. In line with family tradition, his body was cremated, and his father thought it only fitting that John's ashes be spread at the family property in Wollombi, John's final destination.

◆

Dated 16 February 1990, the police report on John's death, written by Constable Sally Dunbar who was in charge of the investigation and signed by four constables at Bondi Police Station, noted that the area where John's body was found was a gay beat, and that gangs had attacked homosexuals there, but bizarrely concluded:

> At this time there is no evidence to suggest the deceased committed suicide or there were any suspicious circumstances surrounding his death. There were no signs of violence on the body and personal property was located on his person. It is my opinion that the deceased fell from the cliff top edge to where he was located. Whether this can be attributed to the deceased's level of intoxication will be clear with the results of the forensic tests.

No matter that the coroner's report, dated 29 November 1989, showed there were a raft of injuries to the body, including fractured ribs, a fractured skull, a fractured clavicle, an extensive series of abrasions, and broken arms and legs. Clearly, most of these injuries would have been caused by the fall itself, but how could the police have ruled out any preceding injuries, particularly as John had a busted lip and a large gash above his eye, more consistent with injuries from an assault, and bruising on the side of his body unaffected by the fall?

And wasn't the position of the body suspicious? John's head, after all, was facing the headland and his legs towards the sea. If he had fallen accidentally, he would have had to twist or rotate his body for it to land in that position. Almost invariably, when someone falls over a cliff accidentally, their head tends to face outwards towards the sea, and their legs inwards. It was almost as if he had been picked up and thrown over. And what about the position of the jersey, halfway up John's torso, suggesting it had been forcibly pulled up? The coroner determined that the body hadn't moved once it hit the rocks. His injuries un-survivable, John had never regained consciousness.

Crucially, at least 30 good crime scene photos were taken of John's body, unlike Ross Warren's, whose car wasn't even photographed or fingerprinted. In a number of the photos a clump of hair can be seen in John's left hand. Those few strands plastered between his thumb and index finger probably held the key to John's murder.

The first inquest into John's death, held in July 1990, lasted just 35 minutes, and stamped the case unsolved, with no clues to his death. The only person who gave evidence was a sergeant from Bondi Police Station. Death by misadventure they called it, consigning the young man's memory to that uncertain catch-all that usually means accidental death, but could also mean suicide. Peter Russell strode out of the courtroom in disbelief and didn't hear from the police again—nor did Dino, who had only been asked to make one short statement within days of his mate's death.

Several weeks after the funeral, Ted Russell had been dutifully handed a set of John's freshly laundered clothes, including the red jersey, gym shoes and $4.60 in change in a big brown paper carry bag.

Ted took that paper bag back to his farm in Wollombi. It was something he intuitively felt might be important in the fullness of time.

The death of his eldest son had blown him to bits, but he knew John hadn't committed suicide. He knew that the boy who had once scaled Ayers Rock and did cartwheels across the dance floor didn't stumble over the side of a cliff in some drunken stupor.

Something terrible had happened to John and it wasn't of his own doing.

Maybe, just maybe, this large brown bag contained some answers about that fateful last hour or two of John's life.

Ted stored it away safely in a locked cupboard, where it was to remain more or less undisturbed for the next eleven years.

3 A DETECTIVE CALLS

It was Sydney's year of glory. The world's biggest international event—the Olympics—was coming to the harbour city in September and from the bleachers of Homebush Bay to the forecourt of the Opera House, Sydneysiders were determined to be on their best behaviour. Everyone seemed to want the expected 700 000 overseas visitors to have a wonderful time, even if it meant giving up the best tables in restaurants, standing cheerfully on sardine-crammed commuter trains and putting up with traffic jams. At the dawn of a new century, the city hadn't experienced such a thrill of anticipation since the Bicentennial in 1988 and the opening of the Sydney Harbour Bridge in 1932.

In the months leading up to those 16 days in September 2000—one year before the shocking terrorist attacks in New York—Sydney wasn't taking any chances. In May, a mock anti-terrorist exercise at the new $31 million Olympic softball stadium was declared an unbridled success, even though it left several thousand dollars worth of damage with doors kicked down, windows smashed and walls flattened. The anti-terrorist squad had been given permission to cause whatever damage they wanted in the name of ensuring that security would be prepared for any tragic turn of events.

On that same overcast afternoon in May, on the other side of the city, Detective Sergeant Stephen Page was sitting in his office at Paddington Police Station—a Victorian maze of a building that in a former life had been a court house—flicking through some letters. After years of working in some of the toughest, grittiest areas of Sydney, placid, well-heeled Paddington, with its avenues of stately terraces, clothing boutiques, art galleries and up-market eateries, seemed another world, even if the sleazy strip joints and gambling dens of Kings Cross were just down the road. It had been a quiet week for Page, with fewer break-ins and assaults than usual, so the balding, barrel-chested 34-year-old was catching up on his correspondence.

There was one very thick envelope poking out from the pile, addressed to the officer in charge of the Missing Persons Unit. Attached to a typewritten cover note were photocopies of a long ream of letters, some dating back to 1998, which had passed through the police bureaucracy, including the then Police Commissioner, Peter Ryan. The letters were from a Kay Warren of the Gold Coast, expressing irritated despair that no inquest had been held into her son Ross's disappearance and probable death back in 1989. The letters had finally wound up at Paddington Police Station because this was where, eleven years earlier, Ross Warren had first been reported missing by a close friend.

All Kay Warren wanted was some basic justice, she wrote in her covering letter. After spending years pleading for a proper investigation, the best she could hope for now, she added, was for her son to be formally declared dead so she could attend to his personal effects. As a parent himself, Page couldn't help feeling moved by this woman's entreaties. Here is a mother, he thought, who hasn't even been given a body to grieve over. No body, no closure. That she had hardly received first-class treatment by the authorities just added salt to a never-healing wound. How can you really get over the loss of a child?

Page had dealt with grieving parents many times before—it was the one aspect of the job that never became any easier. One terrible afternoon, after four teenagers from separate families had been incinerated in a car crash, he had the unenviable task of going from one home to the other, breaking the news to their parents. Telling them their children wouldn't be coming home that night. Then there was the time he had to convince a shell-shocked mother at Mount Druitt that her six-week-old baby, lying motionless in the crib beside her, was really dead from SIDS, and the time he had to take a statement from a grief-stricken Angela Wood, mother of the teenage Anna who died from the combined effects of an ecstasy and water overdose.

Before he called Mrs Warren, Page wanted to find out a lot more about her son's disappearance, so he set about requesting old carbon-copied police statements on the case. When they arrived some days later, a corker of a coincidence jogged his memory. Back in mid 1989, at the same time the newsreader vanished, the then 22-year-old

Page was getting his commission as an Army Reserve infantry officer. Alongside him was a WIN cameraman, James Baker, who went on to become an ABC newsreader in Darwin and a political correspondent for Channel 10. Page vaguely recalled Baker mentioning his colleague's disappearance at the time, and later reading about it in the papers. He now had a reason to contact his old mate, who might be able to provide some insight into Warren's state of mind shortly before his disappearance.

After exchanging pleasantries, Baker, now a political adviser in federal politics, told Page that he had worked directly with Warren on the evening news. He recalled an outgoing, happy-go-lucky person well liked by his colleagues. 'He didn't in the least appear to be depressed, much less suicidal,' recalled Baker. 'Everyone was really shocked by his disappearance—and the circumstances surrounding it, which were all over the papers. Many staff members didn't even know Ross was gay.'

All of which didn't answer the question, what really happened to Ross Warren? Page took a short breath before calling Warren's mother Kay, a woman who had suffered in silence for so long. And he could tell immediately from her tone that she was upset even talking about it; by the end of the conversation, she was in tears.

Yes, she was certain Ross was dead, just as she was sure he didn't commit suicide. Did Kay speak to Ross frequently in the weeks before he disappeared and were his spirits good? Yes, she chatted to him on the phone every Sunday evening, and yes, on the last time they spoke—Sunday 16 July—he seemed his usual self. He was an ambitious boy who was ready to take the next step in his career, she explained. He loved life. He was going places. He wasn't prone to depression, or self-pity. Yes, she knew he was gay, but it wasn't a great issue for him. He knew who he was. Did he discuss his partners or lovers? No, he was pretty private in that regard, although she had met a couple of his boyfriends. But he didn't discuss his sex life.

While Kay believed it likely that Ross had met with foul play, it was just too painful for her to think about. She didn't want to remember him that way. All she wanted now was for her son to be formally declared dead so she could obtain a death certificate and finally sort out Ross's property and personal effects. Why was such a small amount of 'closure' so difficult, she asked?

Good question, Page thought to himself. The vacuum surrounding Warren's disappearance had continued for over eleven years, and it wouldn't be an easy one to fill. He knew from experience these were among the toughest investigations. In a standard murder investigation, police begin interviewing the people closest to the victim and explore any obvious motives, and work outwards from there. More often than not, the offender stands out within an inner or outer circle. When victim and offender are strangers to one another, it's much more of a challenge—doubly so when the case is this old.

Warren. The very name kept buzzing through his mind. It brought back memories of an earlier time in Page's life, to when he was seventeen, collecting supermarket trolleys for Franklins in Winston Hills, only a few kilometres from his home in Blacktown, the gritty working-class suburb in Sydney's west where he grew up with his younger sister.

Page had come to befriend a local delinquent called Warren Hamburger—the name still made him smile—not long out of the Minda juvenile detention centre. So short and diminutive he could have passed for a trainee jockey, Warren had a tough, street-wise exterior but an essentially decent nature.

As Page came from a working-class background himself—his father worked in a factory and his mother in the accounts department of a large company—he understood how easily a kid like Warren Hamburger, from the wrong side of the tracks, could fall in with a bad crowd. Warren had the look of a puppy who had been kicked once too often. The bigger, brawnier Page—then super-fit and thickly muscular from marathon kayak races—had taken to protecting him from the bullies.

One morning Page's little mate walked into the supermarket clearly agitated, explaining that his arch-enemy, Damon Walsh, was after him. 'Walsh means business this time—I know it,' he told Page, his baby-faced bravado momentarily falling away. Page promised to 'sort Walsh out' the next day, after he finished his Franklins shift. But late that afternoon Page was given the following day off, and didn't give much further thought to the tight spot Warren was in. Nor did he see his pal the day he returned to work, so he presumed he was okay. But that night Warren's crumpled body was found in a disabled toilet no more than 50 metres from the glass sliding doors at the entrance to Franklins. He had been bashed to death.

Page was devastated. He felt awful for Warren's family, and angry at himself. He hadn't been there when his mate needed him most. Walsh was later charged and convicted of Warren's murder, but only served a short sentence. Not long after his release he murdered an old man during a break and enter—and then took his own life while in custody. Page took some comfort from the old saying, what goes around, comes around.

Warren's pointless murder was the catalyst that convinced Page he should become a police officer. 'To put vermin like Warren Hamburger's murderer away,' he frequently told himself. Two years later, Page graduated from the Goulburn Police Academy and was immediately posted as a probationary constable to general duties at Blacktown Police Station, his adolescent stomping ground. The fresh-faced nineteen-year-old arrived less than two months after the murder of nurse Anita Cobby in February 1986, a crime so horrific it shocked the nation. Within a couple of weeks, Page was called out to a domestic at the house of John Travers, ringleader of the sadistic band that gang-raped the 26-year-old; the butcher who slit her throat because she could identify him from the tattooed teardrop under his left eye.

On the night of the domestic—only a week or two after John Travers was in custody for Anita Cobby's murder—his younger brother was holding a knife to his mother's throat. Police cars had surrounded the house and Page and his partner helped take the handcuffed thug into custody. The mother had been so terrified she was unable to talk. It was a tough undertaking, but Page was ably supported by a small army of colleagues who were able to get the knife-wielding hooligan under control—and under arrest.

Not so a week later when Page was called out to another domestic at Doonside, after a distressed woman screamed into the phone that her mother—who suffered from a serious mental illness—needed to be immediately readmitted to a psychiatric hospital. As Page and his partner stood in the lounge room, trying to calm mother and daughter down, the son burst in from an adjoining bedroom, pulled out a .22, and promptly shot himself in the stomach. As he collapsed, Page grabbed the gun out of his hand. He then kept him still, got hold of a towel and maintained pressure on the wound to stem the geysers of blood pouring out onto the floor. But then the ambulance staff notified them that they wouldn't approach the house until it was formally declared 'safe' by the Tactical Response Group. In the meantime, Page did what he could in the way of administering first aid and making reassuring sounds to the distressed man— but he had to wait for what seemed like an eternity. And he couldn't ignore the haunted look in the man's eyes, which reminded him of what Vietnam veterans sometimes call the 'thousand-yard stare'—the paralytic shock that comes from seeing the impact that even a low-calibre gun can have on human flesh.

All the while, at the back of Page's mind was the knowledge that the bullet in the man's stomach could just as easily have been lodged in his own chest if that moment of madness had taken a different turn and the gun had turned on him instead. If Page was shaken, he didn't show it, but once he got home that clear autumn night he went for a jog—a very long jog. By the time he had his key in the front door some three hours later, he had mentally dusted himself off. Welcome to the police force, he smiled to himself.

Those first few months in the force offered many light moments, as well—and some rich rewards. What the nineteen-year-old loved about being a cop, he decided, was the camaraderie, the 'esprit de corps' that meant trusting your colleagues and being there for them during the good and the nerve-jangling times. Page also met—and wooed—his future wife at the Police Commissioner's Ball, a pretty sixteen-year-old called Jacqueline, who went on to become a graphic designer in the glamour world of glossy women's magazines. She proved to be his emotional anchor through some of the rough seas to come. The pair were married in 1992 and later had a son and a daughter.

Page had already proved what he was made of in the Army Reserve. The qualities that enabled him to rise to a senior non-commissioned officer—a certain rock-ribbed tenacity and coolness under pressure—were the same attributes that made him a first-class cop. During a six-hour siege on the Central Coast in the mid 1990s, Page acted as a block between the disturbed father who had locked his toddler in the bathroom and was making menacing threats, and the negotiators standing several metres away.

Armed with a shotgun and clad in a bulletproof vest, Page burst into the house after flames started billowing out of the living-room window. Charging through the smoke-filled rooms, Page found the crazed man—and his terrified infant son—cowering in the bathroom. Page helped to save two lives that afternoon—although not before the disturbed father lunged at a fellow constable and tried to seize his gun.

Most cops tend to be cautious, strait-laced people. Although Page was respectful of the rules, he had an independent streak, an ability to think out of left field when he thought the situation demanded it. What struck his colleagues was his willingness to take a gamble in an investigation, particularly when the odds of it being closed successfully were dimming.

More than anything, however, it was Page's decisiveness and unflinching determination that became his trademark—especially when he was moved up to spearhead major murder investigations. And he certainly had to draw on all these inner reserves of strength when in 1998 he was appointed team leader of an investigation chasing the notorious underworld figure Michael Kanaan.

At just 23, Kanaan was head of a crime syndicate responsible for—among a long litany of crimes—the shooting of two footballers outside a Five Dock hotel, a brazen drive-by machine-gun attack on Lakemba Police Station in Sydney's south-west, in which four officers narrowly missed a hail of seventeen bullets, and the wounding of a police officer during a 3 a.m. gun battle at White City tennis complex. Kanaan's handiwork—so Page showed by meticulously linking ballistic evidence—was also behind at least a dozen drug-related 'knee capping' shootings, where victims were shot in the legs. Page was off duty the night Kanaan was finally cornered by the police in a dead-end street at White City; in the spray of shots that followed, the gangster's spine was shattered. In the courtroom afterwards, as Kanaan sat in his wheelchair silent and brooding as he was served three consecutive life sentences, Page received a Crime Agencies commendation for his role in the conviction.

All of which led Page to a promotion as 'investigations supervisor' at Paddington Police Station. It was a cultural shift for Page, and not just because 'posh' Paddington attracted a better class of criminal. The station was located only a few blocks away from Darlinghurst, the gay capital of Australia, and its golden mile, Oxford Street. Unlike some of his former colleagues out west, Page had never had a problem with gay men—he'd had a couple of acquaintances in the Army who were gay, knew a handful in the force, and several more who were industry friends of his wife. Some were 'out'; others kept their sexuality close to their chests. He also knew about the violence against gay people: he'd worked with a police officer who was bashed at a public toilet known to be a beat, and he had gone through the Academy with a redneck who—so it was rumoured—had bashed up a gay man with several others while holidaying interstate.

Prejudice existed in all corners of society, Page understood that—but he'd learned long ago not to stereotype people. And besides, as a member of one of the most unpopular minorities in society—the police force—he knew how it felt to be the object of scorn. Don't judge others, Page had long since learned, and you'll earn more friends.

◆

When Page picked up the phone and began speaking to Ross Warren's old mates, colleagues and family members, a familiar echo reverberated down the line: nearly all of them, from the very moment the newsreader disappeared, believed Ross had been murdered. At no time had the Bondi police treated it as anything other than an odd disappearance or accident at the cliff tops, they complained.

'I never believed Ross committed suicide, and not one of his friends or family thought so either . . . his personality, his outlook on life, was always positive,' said his good friend Craig Ellis. 'You didn't have to be a genius to see that something bad must have happened to him, that further investigation was warranted, that this wasn't just a missing persons case. I raised my suspicions about foul play with the police at the time. After all, people don't usually go for a stroll along the bottom of a rocky cliff face at 2.30 in the morning and accidentally slip. He was probably bashed and pushed into the sea, very near where I found his keys.'

One of Warren's former colleagues, author and television producer and presenter Susie Elelman, agreed. 'There was no way Ross would have committed suicide. He had so many ambitions, was full steam ahead with his life.'

Warren's former make-up artist Christine Jones, who was still employed at WIN, noted: 'He just wasn't the type—he wasn't prone to depression, and he was too much of a wimp to kill himself like that.'

Another friend, hotel owner Rowen Legge, was emphatic: 'I have no doubt that Ross was hoisted off a cliff.'

The other rumour at the time—that Warren had staged his own disappearance—was met with incredulity by all those who knew him well. 'The trail that led to Ross's last sighting was overtly gay, and that would have horrified him,' protested Legge, recalling the television news stories that featured stills of Ross beside video footage of drag queens sashaying down Oxford Street, and newspaper headlines screaming 'Gay Newsreader Disappears'.

'That would have been the last thing Ross would have wanted for his family or his reputation,' Legge insisted.

Page's next step was to call some officers he knew who had been based in the Bondi area at the time, who then led him to those involved in the original investigation. Eleven years after the event, these officers still strongly insisted it was an accident or suicide: Warren had slipped on the moss-covered rocks, fallen into the sea, or had simply thrown himself off the cliff.

Page wasn't convinced. He had long believed that cases such as this should always be treated as homicide until proved otherwise. There were just too many unanswered questions. His natural scepticism turned into outright suspicion when one of the officers mentioned in passing the death of another man at the cliff tops some months after Warren's disappearance, and the murder trial that grew out of the slaying of a Thai man, also at the cliff tops, the following year.

After he tracked down the names of these dead men—John Russell and Kritchikorn Rattanajurathaporn—Page set about obtaining copies of the coronial briefs of evidence surrounding their cases. Long experience had taught Page that sometimes the biggest firepower in a murder investigation comes from being patient and methodical, going over every last detail, and joining the dots. In short, good old-fashioned police work.

When the brief of evidence into the Rattanajurathaporn murder landed in his intray, Page was pleased to see a familiar name at the top of the list of detectives in charge. Back in the mid 90s, Page had worked with Detective Sergeant Steve McCann on an investigation into a series of violent armed robberies on Sydney's North Shore. He remembered the tall, red-haired detective as a thorough, disciplined investigator.

A phone call to McCann proved an eye-opener, and not just on the gruesome killing of the Thai man. McCann seemed to be the only police officer of his time to suspect there may have been a pattern beneath these murders, that gangs were systematically targeting gay men. McCann had been investigating the parallels between the murder of Rattanajurathaporn at Bondi and the culprits behind the slaying of Richard Johnson in Alexandria Park in Sydney's inner east, the so-called Alexandria Eight. McCann said that back in 1991, he had submitted a report on these possible links. But McCann could only take the investigation so far because he was swiftly moved on to other investigative duties.

Page tracked down McCann's report, lodged with the police Modus Operandi section. Although it concentrated on the Johnson and Rattanajurathaporn slayings, he noticed mention was also made of the Ross Warren disappearance and John Russell's death.

Now let's see, thought Page. Ross Warren disappeared on the Tamarama side of the headland, John Russell died on the Bondi side, and the Thai man was murdered smack in the middle, at Mackenzies Point. All gay, all dead within twelve months of one another. A brutal coincidence? It seemed less and less likely. Only one of these murders was solved, and that was thanks to the sterling sleuthing efforts of McCann.

Page wanted to find out more. A lot more. He asked

one of his assistants to do a sweep of the newspaper microfiche and put together a file of press clippings on the Warren and Russell deaths.

This turned up more surprises. Among the torrent of newspaper stories about Ross Warren were a handful that quoted friends and colleagues saying they believed he had been murdered. Even a spokesperson from the Missing Persons Unit—and at least one police officer—didn't dismiss the possibility of foul play.

MURDER FEARS FOR TV WEATHERMAN
```
Police hold grave fears that a missing
television   weatherman   may   have   been
murdered.
```
  The Daily Telegraph, 26 July 1989

TV STAR MURDER FEARED
```
Police fear missing WIN TV weatherman
Ross Warren is dead . . .
  'The circumstances of his death don't
look too good for him,' said Missing
Persons  Bureau  spokesman  Jeff  Emery.
'There's the possibility of murder . . .'
```
  Illawarra Mercury, 29 July 1989

What struck Page was that in spite of the screaming newspaper headlines, the reports on the evening news and all the media attention, the police didn't give Warren's disappearance the ballast of a major case, much less a murder investigation. In fact one police report grizzled about the media's 'getting it wrong' by calling it a murder in the first place. Nor was the 'm' word mentioned in the police reports following John Russell's death, although it was hinted at in one or two newspaper items.

It wasn't until Steve McCann's carriage of the Rattanajurathaporn murder investigation six months later in mid 1990 that the police—or McCann at least—started tossing around the idea that hate gangs were targeting gay men. A couple of newspaper items picked up on McCann's suspicions.

LINK FOUND IN MURDERS

Police stepped up their investigations into a series of Sydney murders over the past three years following a new lead which has linked the disappearance of a 24-year-old Wollongong journalist, Mr Ross Warren, in July 1989, with the unsolved murders of five other men.
The Sydney Morning Herald, 3 April 1991

POLICE REOPEN WARREN MYSTERY

Homicide squad detectives believe a gang of gay-bashers may have murdered WIN TV weatherman Ross Warren, who disappeared from a homosexual haunt almost two years ago.

Sergeant Steve McCann, of the Homicide Squad, said 'sensitive material' existed involving similarities between Ross Warren's disappearance, the death of the two men at Mackenzies Point, and three unsolved homosexual murders in Sydney.
Illawarra Mercury, 7 April 1991

When Page spoke to McCann, the then 51-year-old detective, exhausted after years of back-to-back investigations, was about to leave the force. He wasn't prepared to make a statement about his earlier investigation; he just wanted to get on with his life. But it was clear that like Page, McCann could sniff murder most foul in the deaths of other gay men of the time. In short, a deadly pattern.

So why hadn't this line of inquiry been pursued by another detective after McCann left Waverley Police Station? And why the weak investigative response by the Bondi police to the Warren and Russell deaths in the first place? Did this come down to poor judgment, a vein of homophobia, or simply that their resources were stretched at the time?

It was a question that would no doubt be answered once Page jump-started a new investigation. That is, if he could provide his superiors with enough of a case to open the investigative gates.

4 MURDER ON THE CLIFF TOPS

A leaden sky pressed down on Paddington's colonnaded terraces and church spires; thunder rumbled and the first drops of rain could be heard striking the roof of the police station. Steve Page looked up from the set of crime scene photographs on his desk and gazed at the windows for a few seconds, at the tiny rivulets of water streaming down the panes.

A momentary distraction was welcome. He couldn't help wincing as he examined the shots of the Thai man's drowned body. Kritchikorn Rattanajurathaporn wasn't just bashed to death, he thought. He'd been lynched and left for dead.

Page didn't have a weak stomach. He'd seen hundreds of crime scene photos and videos over the years, many of which made for grisly viewing, including some particularly callous underworld murders. The trademark of the latter was a cool, surgical precision, the victim usually dying swiftly from a well-targeted bullet directed at a vital organ.

But this was different. These butchers had taken mindless pleasure in torturing their victim, prolonging his pain as long as possible—toying with him as a cat does with a mouse in its dying minutes.

Page put the polaroids down. They were among the most hard-to-look-at photos he had ever seen in his career.

Over the next week or so, he pored over the court transcripts of the Rattanajurathaporn murder, in effect the tragic back story to the photographs. What these files presented in total was a grim summary of the events leading up to Rattanajurathaporn's senseless slaying on the cliff tops on that icy Friday night ten years before. A night that might also provide some insight into the shape of the nightmare that also engulfed Ross Warren and John Russell.

◆

Friday 20 July, 1990

In a run-down semi in the inner-city suburb of Redfern, a group of street-hardened teenage boys were knocking back beer after beer and passing around a bong. Outside it was a frosty and cloudless winter's evening, but the cramped living room was warm and cosy—made even more so by the steady thump of rap music. It was still relatively early—8 p.m. on a Friday night—but already the room was brimming with bravado and overconfidence. Briefly, two of the young men squared off drunkenly, but it swiftly turned into a good-natured brawl. Still, as the evening wore on the talk became tougher and the mood darker.

By midnight, brothers Sean and David McAuliffe and their mate Matthew Davis were spoiling for a fight. The two brothers were going out to 'roll a poof', they said. They frequently 'bash gafs' (gays) in the city, they boasted to their mates, but tonight they were heading for Marks Park, where 'there were sure to be gafs'. The Bondi beat, they crowed, was the most active and lucrative 'because all the yuppies that live nearby are wealthy'.

The trio invited the other youths to join them but didn't get even one taker. Seventeen-year-old Sean armed himself with a claw hammer, his sixteen-year-old brother David seemed satisfied with his fists alone, while Davis, sixteen, settled on a stick. Not that any of them needed weapons—the two McAuliffe brothers were skilled in the martial art of tae kwon do and Davis had been in more than his fair share of street fights. And they only ever took on one or two gay men at a time. Just to make sure they didn't get hurt themselves.

Now fired by the fearlessness that comes with the cocktail of youth and alcohol, they set out for Bondi.

◆

The restaurants and pubs along the beachside strip of Campbell Parade were humming. In a Thai restaurant looking onto the beach, a 31-year-old man from northern Thailand, Kritchikorn Rattanajurathaporn, was finishing up his shift, washing dishes. A diminutive scarecrow of a man with big brown eyes and floppy black hair, he was doing casual shifts at the restaurant to help pay for his university studies and the rent on his tiny flat in Bondi. After arriving in Sydney only four months earlier, he had decided to apply to stay in the country after graduating. He'd fallen in love with Australia, he gushed to his mother and sister in frequent letters back home. What he didn't tell them was that as a gay man, he found the lifestyle refreshingly open; this was a place where he could breathe more easily, at last be himself. Where he came from, it was better to keep such matters hidden.

After bidding goodnight to his colleagues, Kritchikorn decided against going straight back to his flat. It was a Friday night, after all, and he wanted to decompress after a long week of work and study. He was in the mood for some company, but a taxi fare to and from the gay bars of Oxford Street would set him back more than a third of tonight's wage.

Where to go? There were no gay bars or venues in Bondi, so he strolled off to the Bondi cliff tops, having heard that gay men hung out there, especially on a weekend night. As he crossed into the darkness of the pathway, his pulse began to quicken; sexually charged situations like these made him feel apprehensive and nervous. So he was partly relieved, partly disappointed, to discover that no-one was about.

Perhaps the cold has deterred everyone, he thought to himself, as he continued on to the lookout at Mackenzies Point, where he intended to turn back. And there, in the moonlight, he made out a slim, thirtysomething man perched on a ledge, gazing out to sea. As he neared, the man turned and gave him a broad smile.

The pair sat there for ten or fifteen minutes, chatting amiably, Kritchikorn in his broken English, Geoffrey Sullivan in his Australian twang, both hunching their shoulders against the icy wind, listening to the heaving ocean battling against the rocks below.

Sullivan warmed to this slight Asian sitting beside him, who regaled him with stories about Thailand, his struggling family who lived in a small village, and his attempts to send some money back home every month. What a soft-hearted man, Geoffrey thought.

The din of the waves crashing against the rocks below was suddenly punctuated by the sound of approaching footsteps on the footpath. Geoffrey turned his head to the left and saw a group of teenage boys emerging from the darkness. Deep in the pit of his stomach, a muscle tightened. He instinctively knew they meant trouble, and grabbed Kritchikorn's arm. 'Quick,' he croaked. But it was already too late. There was nowhere for them to run, nowhere to hide. Not unless they wanted to jump off the cliff together.

The chilling moment arrived. Eyes wild, Sean McAuliffe roared at Geoffrey to 'give me your jacket and money or I'll kill you!'. Desperately hoping this would assuage his attackers—he could see the glint of a hammer in one of their hands—Geoffrey frantically pulled out his wallet and handed over his jacket. But he had no sooner relinquished them than he was struck in the head. He crumpled to the ground under the force of the claw hammer, and as he lay there, defenceless, Sean McAuliffe laid into him with fists and feet.

Ribs cracked and blood vessels burst in Geoffey's head. His lips, however, remained clamped, as if the wave of pain and terror behind them might come sluicing out. His thoughts clouded over.

Kritchikorn, only a metre or two away, was desperately trying to fend off a volley of blows from David McAuliffe and Matthew Davis. He valiantly tried to throw a few punches back. But how could he when they were taking turns to pin his arms behind his back, winding him with punches and kicks? Amazingly, he managed to break free, staggering down the pathway.

'Go, mate! Get him!' David McAuliffe bellowed at Davis, who took only seconds to overtake his quarry and push him over. Now barely able to stand, Kritchikorn was held up by David McAuliffe, who gestured to Davis to thump him harder.

There was a swap-over. Sean McAuliffe, still thirsty for more blood after leaving Geoffrey lying bleeding and semi-conscious on the pathway, started to bludgeon Kritchikorn further. David McAuliffe then set off to 'finish the fight' with Geoffrey, giving him a few more punches and kicks for good measure. Sean took turns with Davis in holding up Kritchikorn by the arms while the other thrashed into him. Every time he landed a good blow, Sean yelled out 'yeah'.

As they grew weary of meting out their incessant punches and kicks, Kritchikorn was able to break free again. Breathing heavily and crying in agony, he stumbled along the cliff edge. There, either because of the effects of the battering which had left him dazed, or out of fear of being attacked again, he slipped over the edge. Trying desperately to get a grip as he fell, Kritchikorn clawed so violently at a jagged piece of rock that he left his bloodstained palm prints all over it. He was too weak, too shocked to hold his own body weight for more than a few seconds. Wide-eyed with horror, he plummeted down the cliff face.

Davis, cradling his left hand in his right, now tender from the pummelling he had given, turned around and saw that his victim was gone. But neither he nor the McAuliffes bothered to check whether their prey was still alive. Instead, they sauntered back to their car, passing by Geoffrey Sullivan lying semi-conscious in a pool of blood, fighting for his life. Strewn near the edge of the cliff top were Kritchikorn's glasses, a sole from one of his shoes and a single sheet of paper snared in a small shrub, fluttering in the stiff sea breeze.

The thin sheaf of notepad paper was lined with neat, curled characters. It was a letter from Kritchikorn's mother in Thailand.

◆

Back at the house in Redfern, the McAuliffe brothers and Davis washed the blood off their hands. Feeling vaguely queasy, Davis wondered for a moment whether the Asian man was still alive. The McAuliffes, however, appeared relaxed, satiated. They lit up a bong.

As they sucked in the soothing warm smoke, Kritchikorn was vomiting blood on a ledge about halfway down the cliff face. He was unable to move, clinging to life like a small bird whose wings had been crushed. He was semi-conscious, his face smothered in blood, a terrible gurgling sound coming from his insides.

He moved his body slightly to ease the pressure—and searing pain—on one side of his body. But he didn't realise how perilously close he was to the edge, and so he fell again—this time into the churning surf below. As he sank into its murky depths, he gasped for air for a few frantic, final seconds.

And then silence.

The person who was Kritchikorn Rattanajuratha-porn—who only hours before had been happily washing dishes and joking with the cook in a Bondi restaurant—now lay in a watery grave six metres down, his body wedged between two large rocks, his big brown eyes still wide open.

◆

Back at Redfern, the boys finally crashed. Their all-night rampage had left them exhausted. They all sank into a long peaceful sleep. No nightmares. No disturbed awakenings in the pre-dawn darkness.

◆

The following afternoon, a Saturday, a mate bumped into Matthew Davis at a Redfern shopping centre. The eighteen-year-old apprentice butcher sniffed a faint scent of blood rising from Davis's shoes, one recognisably different from the cow's blood he was accustomed to in the coolroom of the butcher's shop.

'What's that blood on your shoes?' he asked Davis.

'From some faggot Chinaman's head . . . we beat up this guy in a park last night,' Davis answered quickly. 'You should've seen this mate of mine, he's an excellent fighter. You should have seen the way he kicks.'

Across town, police divers were plunging into the pounding surf at Mackenzies Point, after two tourists that morning found Geoffrey Sullivan lying on the pathway in a pool of blood. In a breaking voice Geoffrey described the attack to the ambulance officers as soon as they arrived, and asked them about his friend, Kritchikorn. The ambos shifted their gaze up to the half-dozen police who had taped off the bloodied pathway, and who were combing through the nearby scrub. The cops had already found torn clothing, a letter and a single shoe—forming a trail that led to the edge of the cliff face.

Within 30 minutes of scouring the underwater rock face under the Mackenzies Point lookout, one of the divers caught sight of Kritchikorn's horribly mangled body. The next day, an autopsy was performed at Glebe morgue. Kritchikorn's face was so disfigured with gashes, pockmarks and horrendous bruising that he looked as if he'd been in a bomb blast.

The post-mortem concluded Kritchikorn died from the combined effects of a violent assault and drowning. So horrific were his head and spinal injuries that even had he survived, he would probably have been left with serious brain damage and perhaps paraplegia.

Across town, in the south-western suburb of Campbelltown, Matthew Davis wrote a letter to his fifteen-year-old girlfriend, telling her how he had gone 'faggot bashing' the previous weekend. Later that week, at a party in the outer western suburbs where he lived, he bragged to some mates: 'Bondi is where all the faggots hang out. Me and me mates have been showing the gays who's boss.' He laughed as he described how his arms and shoes were splattered with blood during the attack last Friday. 'We beat him up and robbed him and then threw him to his death,' he boasted.

Steve Page again checked the date of Kritchikorn Rattanajurathaporn's murder. Friday 20 July, 1990. Six months after the death of John Russell on Wednesday 21 November, 1989. Almost a year to the day after Ross Warren disappeared on Friday 21 July, 1989. Three deaths grouped by time and place. Three men who, probably on impulse, came to the headland late one night after an evening out, unwittingly placing themselves in the clutches of a band of killers. Had these three men arrived half an hour earlier, or strolled about another part of the headland on that critical night, they might have avoided what seemed like the inexorable march of fate. They would have gone home and slept soundly in their beds, not knowing they had come within a whisker of an early death.

Combing through Kritchikorn Rattanajurathaporn's file, Page noted that at least his life was awarded something the two earlier deaths weren't: a skilled murder investigation resulting in swift convictions.

Three elements made this investigation different. First, a tip-off (the mother of a teenage boy overheard Davis bragging to her son about the slaying after she had read about it in the newspaper). Second, a witness (Geoffrey Sullivan survived to give evidence against his attempted murderers). Third, a competent investigation (led by Detective Sergeant Steve McCann, the first officer to suspect that some of these murders were linked).

In one of those bureaucratic quirks that occasionally happens with policing, this murder came under the control not of the Bondi Police Station, which handled the Warren disappearance and the Russell death, but Waverley Police Station.

Still, the evidence would not have been strong enough to convict the trio had Geoffrey Sullivan not lived to testify. Sullivan was kicked with sufficient force to leave the imprint of the sole of a shoe on his cheek and had suffered post-traumatic amnesia. But he survived to make police statements, take the witness box and see justice done.

Unlike the murkiness that surrounded the disappearance of Ross Warren and the death of John Russell, there could be no mistake this time: this was an out-and-out gay killing. Probably for the first time in NSW, detectives investigating the murder appealed to Sydney's gay community. They distributed hundreds of leaflets in hotels and businesses along Oxford Street, and put advertisements in Sydney's gay papers. In a police press release, Detective Sergeant Steve McCann stated:

> We are looking for help from the community who frequent Bondi at night. They may have been assaulted on the night of the murder or been the victim of an attack previously. We'd like to hear from them urgently, in the strictest confidence, to help identify the culprits.

Matthew Davis was arrested less than a month after the attack, and the McAuliffes a few days afterwards.

Although the McAuliffe brothers flatly denied to the court that they were driven to kill by a hatred of homosexuals, they had a tough time convincing the jury because they had chosen a gay beat and had taken weapons there with intent. Davis, on the other hand, had no problem confessing that it was a gay bashing, telling police the killing was a joint venture, that they had decided as a group to 'go and do a gaf'. They chose Bondi, he added, because 'we knew poofs would be there for sure'. Davis freely confessed to bashing other gay men at other locations across Sydney; the McAuliffes, however, denied this to the court. No matter that they had been identified by other gay bashing victims, and David McAuliffe had been prosecuted for the robbery and bashing of a gay man at Bondi only six months before.

Davis told police that Kritchikorn was 'shambling' towards the cliff's edge and when he next turned around 'the Thai man was gone'. The McAuliffes, too, emphatically claimed that Kritchikorn had fallen off accidentally. All denied administering the fatal blow.

But did Kritchikorn fall or was he pushed? In the recreation of the murder above, based on the statements of the three killers, he fell off the top of the cliff. Investigators, however, believed that an equally likely scenario was that the boys pushed Kritchikorn off, watched him fall to the ledge, and left him there. Davis, after all, was heard boasting that 'they threw him (Kritchikorn) to his death', although this was dismissed by the defence team as adolescent skiting. Forensic evidence couldn't prove the case one way or the other—except to show that Kritchikorn, until that final death coil of falling, trying to grasp the cliff edge and falling into the ocean, had put up a courageous fight indeed.

Whatever happened in those final, terrifying moments on top of the cliff face, the result—Kritchikorn's death—was all the same to the Supreme Court jury, who found the McAuliffe brothers and Davis guilty of murder. They were also found guilty of the malicious wounding of Geoffrey Sullivan. When Justice James Wood brought down his sentencing in August 1992—two years and two weeks after the vicious attack—he summed up Kritchikorn's final moments thus:

> ... Either because of the effects of the bashing he had received ... which no doubt left him dazed, or out of fear to escape this violent attack, he went over the cliff.

While the judge said he didn't want to impose a sentence that was 'crushing' to the youths—one that would reduce their likelihood of rehabilitation—he said the savagery of the attack required a strong penalty:

> The message must go out to all young men that gang attacks on defenceless victims will attract heavy sentences of imprisonment. It must be observed the attack was brutal, cowardly, and entirely reprehensible.

Justice Wood might also have added 'cruelly drawn out'. The main indicators of a homosexual hate crime are the protracted nature of the attack, the perpetrators' level of contempt for their victims and the pleasure taken from cruelly tormenting them. The McAuliffe brothers, who had pleaded not guilty, were each convicted of murder and sentenced to twenty years jail, with a minimum term of twelve years, while Matthew Davis, who had pleaded guilty, was sentenced to nineteen years, with a minimum term of eleven years.

Who were these boys, a trio Page dubbed the Tamarama Three? The McAuliffe brothers had come from a broken home, but both had clean records before the murder. Davis had a minor criminal record, including convictions for break, enter and steal and possessing prohibited drugs. His parents had separated when he was seven, and after a time living with his father in Redfern, he had moved to Campbelltown, where he mixed with a 'somewhat delinquent circle of friends'. A psychiatrist described the boys as having average intelligence, without any signs of psychological disturbance. In a masterpiece of stating the obvious, he described them as 'being susceptible to adolescent peer pressures'.

During the murder trial, the court was told that David McAuliffe had attempted to rehabilitate himself, changing schools after being charged in an effort to continue his education. The court was also told that Sean had developed an 'incredible sense of despair and depression' and was 'racked with guilt over what he had done'. Justice Wood recommended that counselling and training be made available to the youths.

Page was interested to read, however, that while they were in jail, Davis complained that the McAuliffe brothers had 'put the dog' on him for being a police informer. He claimed to be the victim of several attacks and a stabbing attempt. In a sworn statement, Davis admitted to having joined the McAuliffes in about 'a dozen bashings of gay men', mostly at Moore Park and Centennial Park:

> I was used as bait. I would talk to the gay men and make them feel at ease, and they got the impression that I was gay and interested in them. The boys would then come up to us, I would pretend I was scared at first, but when they got close we would bash the gafs. The McAuliffes more often than not had a baton to bash the gafs with, and I

would punch them with fists. They were mostly assaulted until unconscious. If they were conscious you couldn't get the money out of them. To be honest, I wanted to knock them out because I hated gafs at that stage.

Before Rattanajurathaporn's murder, however, Davis recalled only going to the Bondi cliffs once with the McAuliffes. On that occasion, about three weeks before Kritchikorn's death, 'we didn't rob anyone' because 'we didn't see any gays that night'. Chillingly, however, Davis recalled David McAuliffe telling him about another murder at the cliff tops, 'around this time, but before the death of Rattanajurathaporn'. In a later statement to police, Davis alleged:

> David McAuliffe told me 'we bashed a gaf and knocked him out and when he was unconscious, we took his cash and jewellery, and threw him off feet first from a cliff'. David moved his hands as he told the story and indicated he held a hand and foot as the gay man was thrown . . .

Only three friends came to say goodbye to Kritchikorn Rattanajurathaporn. Page read that when the police made their enquiries, they were unable to track down his family and instead had sent correspondence to the Australian Embassy in Thailand requesting that local officials try to locate his mother or father.

But combing through the files, Page found to his dismay that there was no return correspondence to suggest this was in fact done. Because Kritchikorn was new to the country and had few friends, there was little to go on.

Nonetheless, the investigation into Kritchikorn's murder stood out at the time—it was one of the few gay murders that drew a swift, comprehensive investigative response and decisive sentencing.

By comparison, as Page was discovering, the police investigations into the deaths of Ross Warren and John Russell were seriously flawed. By the time Kritchikorn's murderers were behind bars, the Warren and Russell cases were collecting dust in the police archives and were long forgotten by the media.

Which left two big questions lingering. Who killed John Russell? And what happened to Ross Warren?

5 BODY OF EVIDENCE

Steve Page was hitting the phones. He knew there are only three ways you can crack a murder case: by physical evidence, eyewitnesses or a direct confession. In most cases, the first two lead to the third. In his preliminary excavations of the Warren and Russell slayings—for he was convinced they were nothing short of cold-blooded murder—he was hoping to dig up some physical evidence that would in turn reveal a treasure trove of clues.

Crime shows like *CSI* and *Crossing Jordan* always made him laugh, moving as they inevitably do from crime to capture within 60 minutes, the clinching incriminatory evidence usually being a two-minute DNA test, which in real life can take weeks. One of the oldest secrets of the detective world is that intelligence work is more often than not a long, onion-peeling exercise that can last for months, if not years—one that involves art as much as science. And the evidence is only ever as good as the person interpreting it.

Which is why Page had the 30 or so crime scene photographs from the Russell death piled up in front of him. He was prepared to spend hours examining them and combing through the accompanying files. What he wasn't prepared for was the wave of recognition that passed through him when he began to read details about the Russell family. He realised with a thunderbolt that he had probably met John Russell's father, Ted, some years before.

The memories came flooding back.

Six years earlier he had met a genial bloke called Ted Russell in the aftermath of the devastating January bushfires that had blackened huge swathes of bushland in NSW's Hunter Valley, driving vast clouds of thick grey smoke over the suburbs of Sydney and Newcastle. Ted was the captain of the local bushfire brigade at Wollombi; Page and another cop had spent a few days driving around with him to all the bushfire sites, investigating where and how the blazes may have started as part of a Coronial Task Force enquiry. In the course of their investigations, the two cops caught and arrested one man red-handed as he was about to light a blaze.

Page and Ted Russell had immediately hit it off, and shared many yarns and laughs as they drove around. They even had a couple of beers back on Ted's balcony when their work was all done.

But it wasn't those terrible January bushfires that were now playing on Page's mind. It was the memory of Ted mentioning that one of his sons had died. The old man firmly suspected he'd been murdered, even if the cops didn't see it that way at the time. Page remembered feeling a strong pang of sympathy for the old bloke, but didn't think it was right to pry too much, so he didn't press for many details. But he did recall Ted telling him he had lived in Bondi for most of his life, and that he had raised his family there. And had two sons.

Page hoped it wasn't the same Ted Russell, but had to find out one way or the other. He didn't have Ted's address or phone number, nor did he have John's birth certificate to confirm the full name of his father. So he checked the White Pages for all listings of Russells in the Wollombi area: to his surprise there turned out to be only one, and Page recognised the voice instantly. After the usual small talk, Page asked the old man if he had a son called John. 'Yes, why?' Ted asked.

The two men had a quiet, serious talk. Page explained that he too felt that John's death was suspicious, especially in light of the Ross Warren disappearance four months earlier, and said he was reopening the investigation. One of the many questions Ted asked—and one of several that Page couldn't answer—was 'how come the media at the time were onto it, but the police weren't?' Ted had kept clippings of several news stories from the local newspapers, and a videotape of a story on gay bashings and murders on *A Current Affair*, in which his son Peter was interviewed at the Bondi cliff tops. This went to air only a week or two after John was killed, and intimated that a gang of youths might be systematically bashing and killing gay men.

So convinced was he that John had been killed, Ted continued, that he had kept the clothes his son had been wearing on the night he died—in the desperate hope they might one day be used as forensic evidence to send the culprit or culprits to jail. Bizarrely, Ted complained, the police had John's clothes laundered and used them to dress a dummy, which they stood in front of Bondi Police Station with a sign, asking anyone with further information to come forward. Perhaps they thought the sight of bloodied clothes would be too much for the public to handle, but why on earth use his real clothes? Surely the evidence had to be preserved?

Page knew forensic evidence such as this can sometimes prove the difference between a conviction and an unsolved crime. He was furious the police had the clothes laundered—even before the age of DNA technology, there could have been invaluable forensic evidence harboured in the threads of his jersey, perhaps a fibre from his attacker's clothing, a hair or even splotch of blood, smudged in with his own.

When he spoke about his son John, it was clear Ted Russell had never got over his death. Father and son had been close—they normally chatted on the phone at least once a week. Yes, John was gay, but he never made a fuss about his sexuality, Ted explained. If he was sitting in front of you now, you probably wouldn't have spotted him as being gay. 'He was a regular kind of bloke who enjoyed fishing, footy and weekends away,' Ted said. John had the ease of a man comfortable in his own skin. 'He was the type of bloke who would give you the shirt off his back.'

Ted agreed to visit Page at the station, said he would bring down the videotape and the press clippings, and gave him his son Peter's number. 'He was very close to John,' said Ted, 'and was as angry as I was about the initial investigation. It's not an easy thing to live with.'

A few days later, Page spoke at length to Peter, who recalled a man who could look after himself. 'Being typical brothers, we had disagreements about different things over the years and on a few occasions came to blows,' Peter recalled. 'The last time this happened was about four months before he died. I had a lot of difficulty controlling him and I am six feet one and weigh 75 kg. We both ended up with nosebleeds and black eyes. He was pretty strong and threw a pretty good punch for a bloke his size.' John had good street smarts, he added. 'He could have defended himself against one or two, but against a pack of six or 10? No-one can do that.'

Page was deeply moved by these reminiscences of a much loved son and brother. Determined to act, he set about putting the formal paperwork into place for an investigation, nominating the class of offence as 'suspicious death' in his request forms to Field Services. Next he organised meetings with his local crime manager Terry Dalton and region commander, Dick Adams. After outlining the scale of the job ahead, both men recognised that a significant investigative response was required. Adams recommended that Page be allocated six detectives to assist him in the investigation. A very good result, all things considered, and Page was very pleased.

Nonetheless, he knew hard choices would have to be made on which investigative paths to follow—the top police brass, with an eye to their budget sheets, could arbitrarily reduce the speed and breadth of an investigation, smash detectives' overtime at a crucial stage in their sleuthing, or fail to resource a job with the equipment it needed. Unless he worked out a clear modus operandi—with clear parameters—Page knew he would be in for a demoralising time, unable to fill vital holes as his investigation evolved.

He also knew that the buck ended with him. At a time when one in three NSW police had less than five years experience, it wasn't always possible to delegate major jobs to young police officers, however talented and enthusiastic, putting a heavier burden on those left to run the investigations. So Page set about doing his homework—carefully examining what had already been turned up in earlier investigations, in everything from phone taps to crime scene photographs.

Meanwhile, several big questions about the investigation continued to hover over him like a storm cloud. If Warren was murdered, were the same group of killers also responsible for slaying John Russell? Or was Russell's murder perpetrated by a different set of killers, with no connection whatsoever to the first? It's just as likely, he thought to himself, that the answer lay somewhere between the two scenarios—among the group who killed Warren may have been one or two, or more, involved in the murder of Russell, and perhaps other gay men.

◆

A week or so later he was sitting at his desk with the 30-odd colour polaroids of John Russell's body laid out before him, taken by the crime scene detectives on the morning John's body was found. Page was studying each photo carefully, searching for clues in the surrounding scene of rocks and scrub. But his eyes kept coming back to the body, lying belly-down in a pool of blood.

There was something not quite right about it.

Page studied the position of the head. If Russell had accidentally fallen head first off the edge of the cliff, wouldn't his head be facing out to sea? Instead, it was facing in the opposite direction—towards the headland. It just didn't make sense. Even if he fell backwards, it would be hard to imagine falling into that position, unless he intentionally tried to do so. And who commits suicide by falling backwards?

Page fidgeted in his seat. What was this in Russell's left hand? A tuft of hair? Why on earth would he be clutching a tuft of hair? Unless of course he'd grabbed at someone's hair as he desperately fought for his life. Page studied John's left hand closely. Did this hair belong to the killer? It looked lighter than John's. Page felt a surge of excitement: with the advances in DNA technology since John's death, this small strand of hair was as good as a fingerprint.

Page immediately called a forensic pathologist he highly respected, Dr Allan Cala, at the NSW Institute of Forensic Medicine. A qualified medical practitioner who specialised in establishing the cause of death, Cala was a straightshooter who had helped him in the past. 'Mate, I'd like you to look at some photos,' Page told him, without pre-empting Cala with his own suspicions. 'They're of a guy at the bottom of a cliff.'

◆

A fortnight later, Page received Cala's chilling verdict in an eight-page report, with line drawings of arms, hands, feet, torso and head marking where the injuries occurred. Cala explained, in his customary clinical style, that the position of the body was not consistent with an accidental fall or jump:

The position of John Russell's body, as depicted in the photographs, is unusual. The body is facing towards the base of the cliff, implying if the deceased acted alone, he has been able to twist his body 180 degrees to rest in the position depicted.

Cala also considered the position of Russell's jersey to be suspicious:

> The red jersey is creased to expose the back and lower abdomen of the deceased, suggesting it had been pulled up prior to the fall. I would not expect the clothing to have that appearance had it been in the standard position at the time of the fall.

And the hairs in his left hand?

> There are some brown head hairs on his left hand near the base of the index finger. It would be unusual to find hairs on the hands of a person who has jumped. This finding is suggestive the deceased might have pulled them from the head of another person at the time he fell, implying the presence of another person or persons at the time of the fall.

Of the wounds to Russell's body, Cala noted:

> There are some injuries to the face and hands which are suggestive of an assault. The deceased would not be mobile at all after the fall, given the number and severity of injuries present.
>
> The injuries (overall) were unsurvivable. He would have been immediately unconscious.

But not dead. That would have taken another 45 minutes or so, Cala estimated.

In summary, he wrote:

> The possibility exists that this man has met with foul play and might have been forcibly thrown off the cliff.

Page's head was spinning with those final words: *foul play* and *forcibly thrown off the cliff*. His suspicions now reaffirmed by an independent source, Page went back to the original crime scene report to see if note had been taken of the position of the body and the mysterious strands of hair clutched in the left hand. It was all there in black and white:

> Deceased located on the rock plateau below cliff. Laying face down in a small depression rock. Head located towards the cliff and his feet were pointing towards the sea.
> Strands of hair adhering to one of the deceased's hands. Packet of cigarettes and a green disposable lighter on the rock at the base of the cliff and a number of coins around the body.

If the detectives who first arrived at the scene didn't see a possible murder in how the body lay, why weren't their suspicions raised by the incriminating evidence—the strands of hair, the jersey raised up—that they themselves listed in their report? How could they take note of these things and not at least ask questions?

Whatever the oversights of the past, the support of a leading forensic pathologist on the position of the body, and the suspicion surrounding the hair in John Russell's hand were enough to turn the case into a card-carrying murder investigation. And although it appeared that the investigation into John Russell's death had serious shortcomings, it was positively wide-ranging compared to the investigation following Ross Warren's disappearance.

Page knew that he would have to put Warren's disappearance, John Russell's death and Kritchikorn Rattanajurathaporn's murder into a far fuller context. And as gay murders weren't exactly his usual beat, he asked Sue Thompson, then the police Gay and Lesbian Liaison Officer, and a pioneer in building better relations between the cops and the gay community, to help him out. Thompson had a wealth of research on gay hate crime, had assembled psychological profiles on gay bashers, and had records of bashings and murders dating back fifteen years or more, all believed to have a gay-hate origin.

They had a long, friendly chat over coffee, although the subject matter was hardly cheery. Thompson began reciting a long list of brutal crimes against gay men and lesbians—stories of murder, of lives ruined, of victims being left with lifelong injuries.

'Heterosexual men are usually attacked by one offender; gay men by three to five,' she said bluntly. 'And those three to five attackers are usually teenagers or men in their twenties.'

Thompson handed him a dog-eared copy of 'Out of the Blue—A Police Survey of Violence Against Gay Men and Lesbians'. She reeled off some chilling statistics: more than one in five gay homicides happen at beats, but fewer than one in five victims of bashings or assaults at beats report them.

'That makes gay men soft targets for young thugs,' she said. 'And those young thugs tend to make a bit of a hobby out of it.'

So why do they do it, he asked, already half knowing the answer.

'To prove their masculinity to their mates—the old alpha male syndrome. To show they are not gay, to steal, or simply because they enjoy bashing people up.'

Page needed more information on beats, in particular the one on the cliff tops.

'Beats are usually about quick anonymous sex, but they can vary—some are more about socialising, others have their own rituals, such as at truck stops,' she explained.

'Marks Park at Bondi was a particular kind of beat because it operated only at night. The area is dotted by areas of scrub and caves in the rock face that men would go in after they had picked someone up on the pathway. A gay male would "cruise" another one by looking him straight in the eye and holding his gaze for a second too long, or nodding. Sometimes they might rattle keys to let someone know they are there and interested.'

Thompson's eyes fell on the coffee cup in front of her. 'I've been a Gay and Lesbian Coordinator for some years, and I can tell you I've heard numerous reports about gay men being led off the pathway on the Bondi headland by a decoy, only to be set upon by a gang.'

If the victims were lucky, she sighed, the battering would leave them with bad bruising and a couple of broken ribs; if they were unlucky, lifelong injuries. Or worse.

Thompson's memory was suddenly jogged. 'Back in 1990 we began conducting education workshops in inner-city schools on homophobia and hate-crime prevention. This was because of the string of gay murders at the time, particularly the murder of Richard

Johnson in Alexandria Park in January 1990, followed by the murder of a gay teacher at Cleveland Street Boys High, across the road.

'Anyway, we were doing a homophobia workshop at Cleveland Street Boys, and in one exercise, students were asked to draw a scene of a gay bashing. One group of sixteen- and seventeen-year-olds drew a particularly realistic drawing and chatted about how they went to the Bondi/Tamarama cliffs most weekends for the purpose of "poofter bashing".

'They spoke in enough detail to suggest they were not boasting. What was also noticeable was that a few of the boys were extremely disruptive. If you like, I can dig out some photographs taken of the students on the day—and my debrief, which I recorded on a dictaphone tape.'

So why weren't these crimes reported, Page asked.

'Homosexuality was only decriminalised in NSW in 1984,' Thompson replied. 'This led to a situation for 200 years where police were viewed as the enemy of gay people. That's why gays and lesbians were extremely reluctant to report crimes to police—or at least, anything that would require them to disclose their sexuality.'

And especially in the 1960s and 70s, Thompson added wryly, it was not unknown for the odd homo-hating cop—or cops—to go out and do a bit of gay bashing themselves, with or without their uniforms on. The climate of mutual distrust thus had a long, ignoble history. It was only in 1990, Thompson explained, that the first gay and lesbian liaison officers were appointed, in response to a sharp rise in gay bashings and murders in Sydney after 1988. The NSW police department was finally forced to do something.

'Where did the crime wave occur?' Page interrupted.

It seemed that the hot spot was a geographic arc between Bondi Beach in the east, and the inner-city suburbs of Alexandria and Newtown.

'And what do we know about the likely culprits? What types of youths were they?'

'Young working-class men from broken homes,' she replied. 'Boys from private schools and stable families. All bonded by one thing: a deep hatred of gay men.'

John Russell's suspicious death and Ross Warren's disappearance, Page thought, now had a back story. Sadly, they were probably just the tip of an iceberg.

◆

Back at his desk, Page scoured his reports, looking for crimes that shared similar features—attacks where similar weapons were used, where victims heard the same expressions or accents, where descriptions of offenders seemed to match. He wanted his team to re-examine records of all serious assaults in the area at that time, just in case there were other victims who changed details or circumstances to keep their homosexuality private.

It would be a challenging task. There seemed to be report upon report of serious bashings on the Bondi–Bronte walk and other nearby 'beats' at the time. Only one of the three deaths—of the 34-year-old Rattan-jurathaporn—became a murder investigation, if only because he was with a friend at the time who miraculously survived. At Alexandria Park, only one of the murders had resulted in convictions.

If Page was in any doubt that Sydney was gripped by an anti-gay killing spree between 1988 and 1992, he only had to check the small pile of newspaper clippings from the era, compiled by a colleague, now piled up on his desk. One particular feature article stood out:

> Sydney's gay heartland is in the grip of an unprecedented wave of violent murders and bashings. Teenage gangs, straight from the nightmare world of *A Clockwork Orange*, are terrorising the yuppie eastern and inner-city suburbs.
> *The Sun Herald*, April 1991

The story went on to describe the case of a local resident brutally bashed outside a bookshop on Oxford Street, only five doors from local councillor Clover Moore's office. The victim lay senseless in the gutter for 30 minutes before help arrived. 'No matter how much the police presence is increased,' Moore told *The Sun Herald*, 'the violence keeps continuing. It's horrific.' Australia's most prolific criminologist, Dr Paul Wilson, painted a bleak picture of the upsurge in violence. 'I don't think there is any doubt the situation in Sydney is worse than anywhere else in the country, even on a population basis. I'm absolutely appalled that the views among school kids seem to be so pro bashing gays.'

Once again, Ted Russell's question echoed in Page's mind. 'How come the media were on to it, but the police weren't?' McCann seemed to be the only police officer at the time bullhorning enquiries into the gay-hate killings. And if the mainstream newspapers made mention of the bashings and murders, they were a white-hot topic in the gay newspapers, Page found when one of his assistants did an archival search from the *Sydney Star Observer*.

'Poofter bashing or first degree murder?' ran a headline in the *Star* on 17 November 1989—only six days before John Russell's body was found at the bottom of the Bondi cliffs. 'In Australia, poofter bashing has long been regarded as an amusing, essentially innocent sport,' opined journalist Paul Paech. 'But now, after AIDS, it has turned into something more sinister, something that leaves people with more than a few bruises and broken bones. Today, poofter bashing amounts to first degree wilful murder.'

In the first six months of 1990, according to another story, more than 90 gay bashings were reported in Sydney, and there had been three gruesome, well-publicised gay murders (Kritchikorn Rattanajurathaporn, Richard Johnson and school teacher Wayne Tonks). One young man quoted in another article admitted to being involved in more than 50 gang assaults and robberies of gay men.

Sydney's gay community was becoming increasingly angry and fearful. The escalating violence finally brought a sea of angry protesters that filled Macquarie Street in front of State Parliament—or so a story in *The Sunday Telegraph* reported in mid 1990. Keeping the pressure up, a small group of activists took it upon themselves to splatter red paint over eleven city buildings—including State Parliament, the Downing Centre court complex and the headquarters of Channel 10 and *The Sydney Morning Herald*. Posters were pinned up nearby, proclaiming:

OUR BLOOD RUNS IN THE STREETS AND IN THE PARKS AND IN THE CASUALTY WARDS AND THE MORGUE—WE'RE OVER IT. STOP VIOLENCE AGAINST GAY MEN NOW.

Angry demonstrators took to the streets again in May 1991 after yet another grisly murder, this time of Maurice McCarty in Newtown, which after Darlinghurst was the next major gay hub. Six hundred gay men and women marched down the suburb's main thoroughfare, King Street, blocking traffic and waving placards.

Sydney's gay community was under siege, the *Sydney Star Observer* reported. Self-defence classes were recommended through community groups and inner-city gyms, and a group of gay volunteers—some of them former members of the Army, Navy and police force—began foot patrols along Oxford Street and Darlinghurst Road on Friday and Saturday nights. Something akin to the Guardian Angels of New York's subway system in the early 1980s, this small team of community-conscious volunteers intervened to prevent dozens of attacks, notified police about suspects and performed citizen's arrests.

Some blamed the violence on the increased profile of the gay community in Sydney—as if, by being more open about their sexuality, gay men had no-one to blame but themselves for unleashing the furies of violence. Public morals campaigner Reverend Fred Nile used his position as an Independent in the NSW Upper House to put forward a motion to State Parliament to ban the annual Gay and Lesbian Mardi Gras parade, which was then drawing more than 400 000 onlookers each year and was growing into a significant NSW tourist attraction, adding $50 million to the state economy every year.

The Reverend Nile had long been a bitter opponent of the gay and lesbian festival—his ultra-conservative Christian group, the Festival of Light, had made it their annual rite to picket the parade. So when Nile presented a motion to State Parliament in April 1991 to 'prohibit by whatever means the homosexual and lesbian mardi gras' on the grounds it provoked 'a backlash in the form of violent attacks', his stand was seen as little more than cynical opportunism by many of his colleagues, most notably state Labor MP Paul O'Grady, who was to draw national newspaper headlines later that year when he openly discussed his homosexuality with Jana Wendt on *A Current Affair*.

Once the draft of likely gay-hate murders arrived from Sue Thompson, Page started chasing old briefs of evidence and witnesses. He was determined to leave no stone unturned. He also requested files on all missing persons in the Sydney city area between 1987 and 1992.

What he began to spot from his preliminary reading was a wearyingly familiar pattern: death after death dismissed as accident or suicide when there were intimations of foul play, just by virtue of where they occurred, and that the victims were probably gay or bisexual.

After weeks of work and help from Thompson, Page settled on a final list of probable gay murders in Sydney's inner city and eastern suburbs between 1987 and 1992. Page's list, reproduced on the next two pages, would later be released to the media in the hope of spiking fresh interest in these deaths—and perhaps new witnesses. What he was after, however, were further clues as to what happened to Ross Warren and John Russell. Behind the bald facts of names and dates, Page knew that lives had been extinguished—and families traumatised forever.

GAY HATE MURDER SPREE, SYDNEY 1987-1992

1. *Tuesday January 13, 1987:*
   Raymond Keam
   Bashed to death at Alison Park, Randwick.
   No charges, no convictions.

2. *Wednesday December 28, 1988:*
   William Allen
   Blood-splattered body was found slumped over his bath in his weatherboard terrace home in Newton St, Alexandria. Previously bashed in Alexandria Park.
   No charges, no convictions.

3. *Friday July 21, 1989:*
   Ross Warren
   Disappears into thin air, his keys found at Marks Park, South Bondi.
   No charges, no convictions.

4. *Wednesday November 22, 1989:*
   John Russell
   His body is found at the bottom of cliffs in Bondi.
   No charges, no convictions.

5. *Wednesday January 24, 1990:
   Richard Johnson*
   Bashed to death at Alexandria Park.
   **Three youths convicted of murder,
   five of manslaughter.**

6. *Saturday May 19, 1990:
   Wayne Tonks*
   A teacher at Cleveland Street Boys
   High, found murdered in his flat.
   **Two convictions seven years after
   the crime, one for murder, one for
   manslaughter. The second alleged
   killer walks free upon appeal.**

7. *Friday July 20, 1990:
   Kritchikorn Rattanajurathaporn*
   Found dead at the bottom of cliffs at
   Marks Park, Bondi.
   **Three youths charged with murder and
   convicted.**

8. *Sunday April 7, 1991:
   Maurice John McCarty*
   A 47-year-old head technician with
   the Australian Ballet Company, found
   in a pool of blood in the backyard
   of his Newtown home.
   **A 19-year-old is convicted of murder.
   Later acquitted on appeal.**

9. *Saturday August 22, 1992:
   Cyril Olsen*
   A 58-year-old clerk, found washed up
   at Rushcutters Bay.
   No charges, no convictions.

Surveying this grim list of crimes, any detective with any respect for his sanity would have been tempted to toss it in the too-hard basket. Launching a fresh investigation into the death of Ross Warren and John Russell eleven years after they occurred was daunting enough; exploring any possible interconnections with a string of other gay murders would prove a logistical nightmare for his team.

But there was something about the Warren disappearance and Russell's death that Page couldn't leave alone. And it amounted to much more than just the eerie coincidence of having a mate who had worked with Warren at WIN studios, and having met John Russell's dad some years earlier. It was more to do with the way these men's lives didn't seem to amount to much in the eyes of the authorities back in the late 1980s. Page wanted to achieve justice for these men's ghosts—and some degree of closure for their families who had suffered in silence for so long.

But he was under no illusions about the scale of the task ahead. What he had in front of him was a dark mosaic of murder—one that he would have to meticulously piece together with slow, grinding thoroughness. In April 2001, after months of sleuthing and interviewing relevant parties, Page was allocated a name for the thorny investigation ahead of him: Taradale.

After nearly twelve long years, Ross Warren and John Russell were finally about to receive the kind of investigative response their violent deaths had always warranted.

6 DEAD MEN WALKING

Dusk was creeping up the shutters of what Steve Page called his 'operations room' at Paddington Police Station. This was the nerve centre of Operation Taradale. Crammed into the long narrow room—an antechamber in the old law courts—were three computers and four filing cabinets. Running along the entire length of one wall was a grand, beaten-up wooden desk, actually the old Bar table from the courtroom next door, which Page had 'borrowed'. Smothering most of the desk were bulging piles of folders, containing yellowing coroners' reports, transcripts of tape recordings, police summaries and witness statements, all telling the story of the wave of anti-gay murders that swept Sydney's inner city in the late 1980s.

Out of the nine gay murders on Page's central list, only four—of Kritchikorn Rattanajurathaporn at Bondi, of Richard Johnson in Alexandria Park, Maurice McCarty in Newtown and Wayne Tonks in Artarmon—resulted in trials. Two of the alleged killers were later acquitted; two more were handed light sentences. That left four murders still shrouded in mystery. And killers who have simply melted back into the suburbs or the country.

Steve Page smiled to himself. He knew from long experience that there are few real murder mysteries: only guilty people with dark secrets, witnesses who won't come forward out of fear or misguided loyalty to the killer, or maybe a case that remains unsolved because of a mis-step or two by the investigators, who misread a critical piece of evidence. The unvarnished truth is always out there. Somewhere. The cops score a break and then—whammo—the coldest of cold cases is suddenly on the boil again.

If there was one murder that summed this up—or at least, how killers can unexpectedly appear out of the shadows—it was the slaying of gay school teacher Wayne Tonks in 1990, the one case on his list with which Page had had passing contact. In the mid 90s he was working in the North Side Area Command when Tonks's two killers were suddenly dobbed in to the police, seven years after the grisly murder.

Page again studied his neatly typed list of names—he knew that this death toll might not be final. Who knows how many other gay men, dismissed as missing, had really been murdered, he thought. He looked across at the reams of information in front of him. Poking out of one folder was a report from the Sydney Water Police. It described how, on a December morning in 1990, two rock fishermen saw a body floating in the sea off Mackenzies Point; it was never found or identified. What happened to this person, believed to be a young man,

Page wondered. His life simply amounted to an 'occurrence pad entry' lodged with the Sydney Water Police.

Page put in a call to Sergeant Jeffrey Emery, of the Missing Persons Unit, explained what he had in mind, and organised a meeting. Page found he had a receptive listener when they met up in Emery's offices some days later. From now on, they both agreed, the information required in the analysis of each missing person would include whether the person was homosexual. A simple change on the forms, but one that would make it much easier to track gay hate crimes in the future.

More than anyone, Page knew he was not in a position to reopen investigations into all the unsolved gay murders on his list. He had to be careful not to stray too far from the terms of the investigation into the Warren and Russell deaths, already proving to be a snowballing task in itself. In sorting through coroners' reports and witness statements from these other solved and unsolved cases, he was looking for common threads that might throw light—and hopefully leads—on the deaths of the newsreader and the barman.

What all these murders formed, in a way, was a collection of ghost stories, made up of gay men—brothers, sons and fathers—all unknown to one another but sharing a common tragic fate ... and perhaps some common killers.

If there were *any* links between these murders, they might be tucked away somewhere in these folders, perhaps in a throwaway line in a police statement, a half-submerged fact brought before the courts, a tantalising lead. It took Page several weeks to pore over the details of each case and, as he did, he gradually came to feel he knew these men—at least as well as most people know their neighbours or the guy who works in the local shop. But the part that stayed with him, sadly, was the final, brief chapter in their lives. Page had been in the force long enough to know how swiftly a stable, hard-working life can be smudged out.

William Allen, 51, former school teacher
Murdered at Alexandria Park, Alexandria
Wednesday December 28, 1988
No charges, no convictions

William Allen was at death's door. Breathing in shallow gasps, with a broken jaw and a deep gash over his left eye, the impish, slightly paunchy 51-year-old gingerly lifted himself up from the dew-covered grass where he'd been lying semi-conscious for well over an hour. Sharp pains racked his chest as he squinted at his watch. It was nearly 3 a.m. His left hand, throbbing from where a Phillips head screwdriver had been thrust into it, was curled up in a claw, useless. He stood, unsteadily, only three or four metres from the toilet block in Alexandria Park where he had been brutally bashed. Cradling his jaw with his right hand, Allen—a former teacher at the prestigious boys' school Newington College—staggered across the street, now deserted of traffic.

A middle-aged couple, about to cross the road and aghast at his bloodied state, offered to call an ambulance, but he waved them away. All Allen would mutter was that he had been attacked by a group of teenage boys in the park. And he just wanted to get home.

Which is exactly what he did, staggering, stumbling back to his neat weatherboard terrace in Newton Street in the pre-dawn darkness, a good ten minutes walk away. Disorientated by the pain, perhaps he didn't realise that his internal injuries were grave, that only urgent medical attention could save his life.

Either that or he had already given up, a broken spirit whose final wish was to die at home, beside the two spaniels he loved.

There was not a soul in his small, leafy street—a mishmash of nineteenth-century terraces and 1970s units—as Allen reached the sanctuary of his front yard. He fumbled with his keys, leaving a small trace of blood on the door jamb as he brushed past. The white push-button phone on his living room table was ignored as he made his way to the kitchen for some water.

He made no desperate calls for an ambulance, no angry calls to the police. Not even a distressed appeal to a friend. Allen didn't even make sufficient noise to alert his neighbour, with whom he was on good terms. Instead, he staggered from room to room, quietly moaning and weeping, leaving small drops of blood wherever he stepped. And as every precious minute passed, he was nearer the end.

Death came just as dawn was breaking. Allen finally collapsed in the bathroom, but attempted in one last show of strength to pull himself up on the side of the bath. As he did so a spurt of blood came out of his mouth. His face was already smudged with blood and tear marks.

Allen might have lain there for days, maybe even weeks, had not a handyman dropped by the following morning at 7.30 to finish off some small carpentry jobs and collect his money. When Allen didn't answer the front door or back door, he strolled down the side and peered through a bathroom window. Through the frosted glass he saw his client's half-naked body slumped over the claw bath. When police arrived half an hour later, Allen's two pet dogs were guarding the bathroom door, whimpering.

To this day, no charges—let alone arrests—have been made as a result of his killing. The case drew scant attention, barring a few paragraphs in the local newspapers. Little is known about Allen's movements earlier that evening. He had probably eaten at home: a lone dinner plate, and single knife and fork, lay unwashed in the sink; a saucepan, containing two potatoes, sat on the stove.

Questions loomed in Page's mind. Did Allen meet his killers at Alexandria Park, while cruising the beat late at night? He was, after all, a regular at the park, more often than not taking his dogs for a walk there. Or was he lured to his death, as he had unwisely left his phone number on a cubicle wall in the toilet block? As he didn't take his dogs with him that night, was this a more likely scenario?

From the police reports, neighbours and friends described Allen as a kind, friendly man who had lived in the house for about five years after his brother had moved out. He tended to keep to himself, but was known to help a couple of elderly relatives with their groceries. Now that the renovations on his home were complete, he was planning on going away the following week on a holiday. It was, after all, just three days after Christmas.

Page came across other far less saintly stories, however. There was Allen's predilection for teenage boys, his habit of haunting beats, and a neighbour's report of occasional visitors late at night. Allen was also being investigated for having sex with an under-age boy.

None of which, of course, justified him being bludgeoned to death.

Richard Johnson, 33, office worker
Murdered at Alexandria Park, Alexandria
Wednesday January 24, 1990
Five convicted of manslaughter, three with murder

It had been a loud, boisterous game of basketball between eight teenage boys—most of them students at Cleveland Street Boys High—on a hot summer's night. One of their favourite hang-outs during the school holidays was this basketball court adjoining Alexandria Park. Due back at school that week, they were making the most of their last days of freedom. In the park opposite, during the winter months, they played footy with many of their mates and knew all about the toilet block situated on the northern side. After nightfall it became a poofters' hang-out. A gay beat.

After the game they ambled across the road to the park, and headed straight for the toilet block. One selected a telephone number scribbled on the cubicle door and proceeded to call it from a public phone box nearby, while his mates listened in, sniggering. The number belonged to Richard Johnson, a slim, darkly handsome 33-year-old New Zealander who lived in Coogee; the boy invited him to come to the park for sex, enticing him with statements such as 'I like to give head jobs'.

Johnson took the bait, arriving at the agreed time—10 p.m.—after parking nearby, and walking across the same thatch of grass where William Allen was felled only a year before. Perhaps sensing danger, Johnson had no sooner stepped into the toilet block than he attempted to leave. Alas, it was already too late.

The next horrifying few minutes were summed up in a dispassionate three-page report by the trial judge. Page absorbed each line:

> The eight young men, who had been waiting at the school grounds at a point where they could observe the toilet without themselves being seen, ran towards the toilets whilst their intended victim was inside the building, and when he emerged seven of them set upon him without mercy. One punched him heavily and without warning to the jaw and he fell to the ground. He was still conscious as most of the group assaulted him in various ways. At least two of them stomped with one heel on the right side of the victim's head above and behind the ear, causing a subarachnoid haemorrhage and almost certainly unconsciousness. Many of them kicked him in the head and trunk. One at least jumped on the victim's right chest as he lay on his back, landing with his full weight on both knees. One or more such impacts caused multiple rib fractures and the liver injury which was the actual cause of death.

The attack lasted no more than three or four minutes, but long enough for his liver to be split into two. In the words of one assailant, Richard Johnson 'didn't stand a chance'. Some of his attackers mocked him with 'why be a fucking poofter?' and 'there's no point being a poof', laughing as their helpless victim desperately pleaded with them to 'leave me alone, I'm sorry I'm gay'.

Their savage assault over, a couple of the boys rifled through Johnson's pockets, and divided up the booty among the others, which amounted to a few dollars each. They left Johnson lying on a patch of grass, bleeding to death. A man walking his dog the next morning saw his beaten body, unconscious and curled up, in a pool of blood a few metres from the toilet block. He immediately called an ambulance, but Johnson died in hospital some hours later. Perhaps mercifully for him, he never regained consciousness.

After a tip-off, Johnson's killers were charged within a month of his death, and brought to trial later that year. Three youths were convicted of murder and five of manslaughter, with two handed maximum sentences of eighteen years.

The presiding judge accepted that an extreme hatred of homosexual men had been behind the slaying, but expressed irritation at newspaper stories that suggested some of the boys were involved in earlier bashings of gay men, which might bias the jury. Never mind that these media reports were true. After some judicious cross-checking with other files, Page found that at least three of the boys had been implicated or identified in a long string of bashings.

Most disturbingly, in a police statement some time later, one of Johnson's murderers implicated two of his co-accused in the earlier murder of Allen, alleging they had bragged about the killing, even describing a screwdriver they had used to puncture his hand. On Steve McCann's initiative, Johnson's killers were re-interviewed in 1990 as part of renewed enquiries into that earlier death, but the investigation faltered not long after the jail sentences were doled out. As in so many cases, there simply wasn't enough hard evidence to bring the matter to court.

If the staff and students at Cleveland Street Boys High were under pressure during the murder investigation and the lurid newspaper headlines that followed the death of Richard Johnson in early January, it was to turn into absolute heartache when one of their most popular and respected teachers was found murdered at his North Shore apartment only four months later.

Wayne Tonks, 32, school teacher

Murdered at his Hampden Road, Artarmon, unit Saturday May 19, 1990
One convicted of manslaughter, one with murder

Wayne Tonks was bound to a dining chair with thick green masking tape. He couldn't see a thing; he couldn't cry out for help. A few minutes earlier, after bludgeoning him with a mini baseball bat, his two attackers had used the masking tape to plaster over his eyes and mouth. He could hear them moving about his unit, emptying drawers and slamming cupboard doors.

Just when he thought it couldn't get any more terrifying, he felt something being pulled over his head. He breathed in, but what felt like plastic was sucked into his nostrils. As he frantically tried to break free of the bindings, his chair fell to the floor.

It took only two or three minutes for the life to drain from his body.

Two days later, police busted through Tonks's front door after his colleagues at Cleveland Street Boys High, worried that the normally punctual school teacher hadn't turned up for work, alerted the authorities.

A social science teacher who also taught drama and coached rugby, Tonks—or as he was affectionately known, 'Tonksie'—was widely respected by staff at the school. Students, according to one former teacher, 'would line up for his lessons'. No small feat, as Cleveland Street Boys—located only ten minutes from Redfern's notorious crime hot spot The Block, and circled by the still fiercely working-class neighbourhoods of Alexandria and Waterloo—had the reputation of being the toughest school in the state. In its glory days, this classic 'school of hard knocks', with its sandstone walls and Victorian spires, spawned some of Australia's most esteemed sporting figures, including soccer legend Johnny Warren, Australian test cricketers Charlie Kelleway and Alan Kippax and Australian Wallaby Nick Shehadie. Perhaps its most famous non-sporting graduate was Sir Garfield Barwick, former Chief Justice of the High Court. By the late 1980s, however, one staff member was describing the school as a 'battleground' in which teachers who 'couldn't cope with the strain left early'.

But Page also knew that the school was notorious for a different reason: a handful of its students had slaughtered Richard Johnson, and there was suspicion that some may have been involved in the earlier death of Allen. When police learned that Tonks was gay, they immediately suspected it was connected in some way to the recent Johnson murder, and set about re-interviewing friends of the suspects and students at Cleveland Street Boys High. It was a logical investigative route, and Page could understand why they followed it. Tonks had taught three of the boys convicted of Johnson's murder.

In a sad irony, he'd even counselled a couple of them after they were charged.

Small wonder then that the school teacher was guarded about his homosexuality, and feared for his safety—a concern he had expressed to colleagues. A slight, short man, Tonks didn't go to the bars of Oxford Street, largely for fear of being spotted on the strip by colleagues or students. Paradoxically, though, he frequented beats, and had got into the reckless habit of leaving his phone number on toilet walls and doors. To reduce the obvious dangers of running into any of his students, he only did this in areas well away from where he worked, avoiding the high-risk inner city and Eastern Suburbs.

Among the places where he scribbled his number was a public toilet outside Stanton Library in the high-rise jungle of North Sydney. A sixteen-year-old boarding school student, Benjamin Andrew, who was studying at the library during the Easter holidays of 1990, saw Tonks's name on the wall and called him late one Saturday night a couple of weeks later. He told Tonks he was unsure of his sexuality and needed someone to talk to. Andrew, who could come and go as he pleased because he had a self-contained flat at the back of his parents' home in Castlecrag, met Tonks at North Sydney railway station. They then went back to Tonks's unit.

No matter that the boy was just sixteen, at that time two years below the age of homosexual consent in NSW. No matter that this was at the height of the investigation into Richard Johnson's murder and Tonks knew first hand what dark deeds teenage boys were capable of. But for whatever reason, the teacher threw caution to the wind.

What happened at the Artarmon unit that night—and more to the point, at a second meeting there—is still a matter of fierce conjecture. Andrew claimed Tonks plied him with alcohol, played pornographic videos, offered him a massage—and then sexually assaulted him. Two weeks later, feeling totally abused, he returned to Tonks's flat with his best friend from school, Peter Kane, to let him know 'how he felt about the way he had been treated'.

Once inside the unit with his accomplice, Andrew struck Tonks on the back of the head and with Kane's assistance tied his arms and legs to a chair and taped his mouth and nose. Their victim now defenceless, Kane put a plastic bag over Tonks's head, but Andrew didn't see him tape the bottom of it, cutting off the air supply.

This was how Wayne Tonks met his cruel fate—at least according to the courtroom testimony of Ben Andrew that Page was combing through. Peter Kane's version of events, however, could have almost belonged to a different crime. According to Kane's testimony, both boys met Wayne Tonks and another man in Miller Street, North Sydney, and Tonks later invited them back to his apartment, where they were allegedly supplied with alcohol, probably spiked, and shown pornographic videos. Tonks then allegedly raped both boys. Two weeks later, according to Kane, the two boys returned to the flat for the revenge attack, but didn't intend to kill Tonks, just give him, in Andrew's words, 'the fright of his life'.

Kane couldn't remember who put the plastic bag over Tonks's head, nor who taped it to his neck. Fingerprints on the plastic bag, and the tape attached to it, were later found to match Kane's. Andrew's fingerprints were only found on the tape securing Tonks's body.

Whatever the real truth behind Wayne Tonks's murder, both boys managed to keep their guilty secret for more than seven years without prosecution. None of the fingerprints in Tonks's apartment matched those of any of the suspects surrounding the Richard Johnson murder—in fact, to the surprise of the police, there didn't appear to be any connection with Cleveland Street Boys High at all. The cops were mystified: the murderers—and they knew there were at least two from fingerprint dusting—had simply come out of nowhere and disappeared.

Ben Andrew wasn't good at keeping secrets, however. In a heated exchange with a teacher at St Gregorys' a year later, he boasted that he had killed a man who had 'done something to him'. Twelve months later, he repeated the same story to a cook at the school while on a school excursion, but the two staff members failed to contact the police.

Life inevitably moved on. Peter Kane met a woman, moved in with her, and in January 1994 married her, asking Ben Andrew to be his best man at the wedding. He toiled away at his job and sired two children. It was only after Kane's marriage crumbled in 1997, and the couple became involved in a bitter custody battle over their kids, that the truth finally came out. Kane's wife went to the police with the dark secret that her husband had confessed to her in an intimate moment some months after their wedding.

In a somewhat controversial decision, the two men were given separate trials in April and May 1999, which resulted in radically different outcomes—Andrew was convicted of manslaughter, and Peter Kane of murder. Kane was sentenced to ten-and-a-half years in jail, while Andrew, after a successful appeal on his conviction, walked free.

Page rang one of the detectives involved in the Tonks investigation, Matt Perry. There were a minefield of moral and legal issues in the case, Perry explained. Even if Andrew did not perform the killer action of putting the plastic bag over Tonks's head, even if he didn't realise Kane had taped it to the dying man's neck—as he claimed in court—was he not as morally responsible? Both boys, after all, took the baseball bat, masking tape and plastic bag to the unit. Both boys walked out the front door leaving a man gasping for breath.

And then there was the little matter of provocation versus self-defence. Did Tonks sexually assault both boys, or only Andrew, or neither? Tonks was obviously not able to defend his name while it was being blackened in the courts—his grieving family were left to bear the brunt of the claims against their much loved son and brother.

Former detective Malcolm Smith, who spent seven years investigating the Tonks murder, found it implausible that the slight-framed Tonks—who weighed less than 70 kg—could overpower and hold down the thickset Andrew, much less the taller, strapping Kane. 'I felt at times I knew the victim better than his own family and to suggest that Wayne, a well-respected high school teacher, would rape someone—there's no way that would happen,' he told ABC reporter Chris Masters on *Four Corners*.

Police prosecutors thought a more likely scenario was that Andrew had sex with Tonks, perhaps under some persuasive pressure from the older man. How much or little physical coercion was involved is impossible to know. Later, overcome with guilt and feeling manipulated, Andrew plotted a path of vengeance with his good mate Kane. That something *did* happen at Tonks's apartment on that first visit—something traumatic enough to set Andrew on the tragic path he followed—is beyond doubt. Two months after the murder he fronted up at an AIDS clinic in Sydney's Surry Hills for a HIV test, accompanied by Kane. Only Andrew asked for a test, and he made no mention to the counsellor of being assaulted. If he was raped in the fashion he claimed—plied with alcohol and overpowered—why did he not go to the police? Shame? Humiliation?

There were other unanswered questions. Was Tonks, as Andrew's defence team insisted in court, a paedophile? That he was gay, and pushing the envelope by inviting sixteen-year-old boys into his home and giving them alcohol, is certain. Friends testified that Tonks had a predilection for young men—early twenties down to late teens—but there was no suggestion he ever had sex with anyone under sixteen. As the homosexual age of consent was then eighteen (and for heterosexuals sixteen) Tonks could have, as Andrew's defence team branded him, been called a child molester. But if he had, for argument's sake, invited a sixteen-year-old girl into his apartment and given her alcohol, would the defence team have gone down the path of painting him as a paedophile? An opportunistic sleazebag, certainly, but a paedophile?

Regardless of the true sequence of events on the crisp Saturday evening of May 19, 1990, Page read on to discover that Ben Andrew was clearly a haunted man for years afterwards. He may have walked free, but his life soon started to spiral downwards, via a cocktail of alcohol, drugs and heavy partying. In early 2003 he didn't turn up for work and his employer later found him dead in his flat. The coroner's verdict: 'pneumonia'.

Peter Kane is due for release in 2008, having lost more than a decade's time with his children. Tonks's family imploded under their grief: in the years since his death, both his parents and his sister have all passed away.

No, the Tonks murder didn't fit the pattern of other gay murders of the time, Page decided. It wasn't a gang killing; it wasn't perpetrated by a bunch of youths with a history of serial gay bashing; it wasn't about killing for no other reason than the victim was gay. Nor was it part of a dark tapestry threaded to other bashings and murders. No, this was a one-off 'revenge' murder, a result of a tragic convergence of events.

Wayne Tonks did, however, share two fundamental things in common with Richard Johnson, Ross Warren, John Russell and Kritchikorn Rattanajurathaporn. He was gay, and he was a featherweight of a man, both of which made him an easy target. In the rough and tumble of the street or the public park, gay bashers and killers carefully pick their victims, singling out those smaller and slighter than themselves. Men built like front-row forwards, or those who look like they might be handy with their fists, tend to be bypassed.

But there are always exceptions to the rule, as Page soon found.

John Russell at three, putting on his best smile for his proud mum, who was behind the camera.

'John loved animals,' according to his father Ted Russell, who took this shot of his 15-year-old son with the family dog.

As a gregarious 22-year-old with a cheeky sense of humour, John Russell earned good tips at Oxford Street clubs such as The Tropicana in the late 1970s. Here the barman is relaxing at his home in Bondi in 1979.

Snapped at a celebratory dinner in the winter of 1989, this was the last photograph of John Russell taken while he was alive.

Promotional shot of Ross Warren taken shortly after joining WIN TV as a weatherman in 1987.

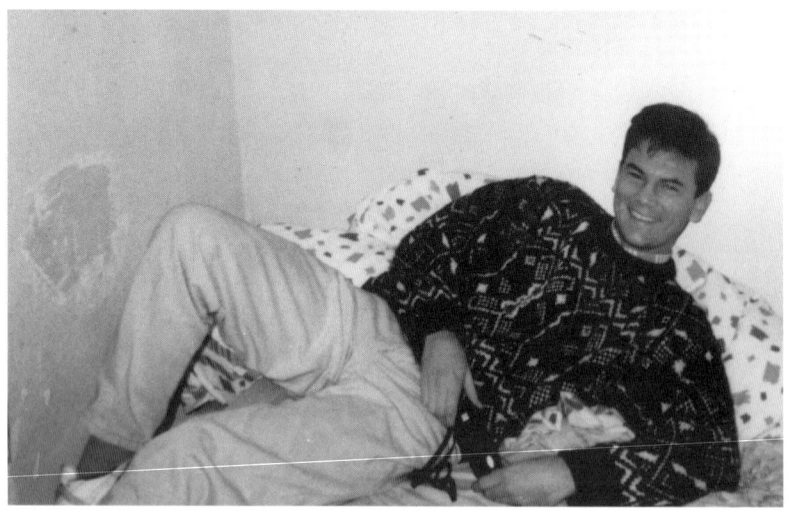

Ross Warren at home in what friends described as his 'dark and dinghy' one bedroom apartment in Wollongong, May 1989. At the time of his death, the newsreader and weatherman was making plans to move to Sydney.

'He had a happy self-confidence, but Ross was never arrogant,' according to friend Rowen Legge, who took this snap after a few laughs at a dinner party in the summer of 1988/89.

Ross Warren with make-up artist and friend Christine Jones, on set at WIN during a fundraiser, late 1988. 'Ross was a bit of a larrikin; he enjoyed playing practical jokes,' Jones recalls fondly.

Gilles Mattaini is all smiles for partner Jacques Musy, who was behind the camera for this holiday snap, taken in Bali in 1984.

Jacques Musy and Gilles Mattaini in Paris in 1983, shortly before their departure for Australia.

Gilles Mattaini in the yellow spray jacket he always donned for his cliff side walks, early 1985. Mattaini would stroll for hours listening to French pop music on his Walkman.

Gilles Mattaini at home in Ramsgate Avenue, Bondi, in the winter of 1984. 'The only thing he loved more than beating you at cards was spending a day at the beach,' according to Mattaini's long term partner Jacques Musy.

A proud, fresh-faced Constable Stephen Page immediately after his graduation from the Goulburn Police Academy, April 1986. Within two months, he would be seconded to one of Sydney's toughest police stations.

Detective Sergeant Stephen Page made many visits to the cliff tops during his 3-year investigation with witnesses and victims. 'For the families of the dead, this is a place of tragedy,' he says.

Page near the spot where Thai man Kritchikorn Rattanajurathaporn was driven to his death. 'Kritchikorn loved Australia and wanted to stay,' says Page.

Only an hour or so before he was bashed to death, Thai national Kritchikorn Rattanajurathaporn was working as a kitchen hand in a Bondi restaurant.

Raymond Keam, a Department of Main Roads technician, was a top level martial artist, but it wasn't enough to save him from a gang of killers.

New Zealander Richard Johnson, who was lured to Alexandria Park, set upon and left for dead. The 33-year-old never regained consciousness and died some hours later in hospital.

After teachers at Cleveland Street Boys' High alerted police that their colleague Wayne Tonks hadn't turned up for work for two days, the front door of his Artarmon apartment was busted in. Police found the 32-year-old bound to a chair with a plastic bag over his head.

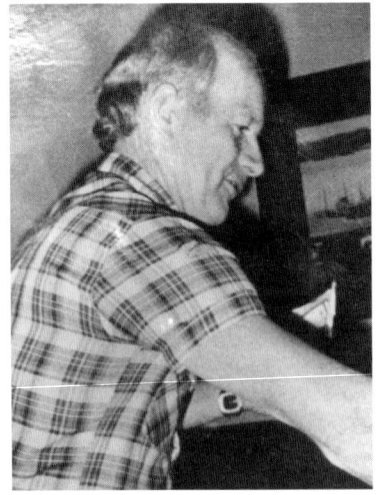

When neighbours heard cries over their backyard fence and went to investigate, they found Maurice McCarty, a technician with the Australian Ballet, lying in a pool of blood.

Raymond Keam, 43, Department of Main Roads technician

Murdered at Alison Park, Randwick
Tuesday January 13, 1987
No charges, no convictions

Tall and leanly muscular, Raymond Keam had the kind of body most men envy. Around his neck he wore a silver medallion, declaring him to be a member of the Zen Chi Ryu group, an elite band of black-belt karate experts specialising in full-contact, no-holds-barred sparring, arguably the most street-savvy martial art of all. But Keam knew better than anyone that if you're hopelessly outnumbered, you don't stand a chance, no matter how strong a fighter you are.

On a clear night in January 1987, outside a toilet block in Alison Park, Randwick, Keam was savagely beaten and left to die. Nearby residents, long accustomed to seeing and hearing assaults in the park—there had been at least eight attacks there in the previous twelve months—heard a commotion at about 2 a.m., but failed to call police because it had happened so many times before.

Keam's body was found at 6 a.m. on the other side of the park by an elderly woman walking her dog. His pockets had been turned inside out, and his wallet stolen, but still hanging around his neck was the silver medallion. Translated, the Japanese inscription on it read: 'The path of the Zen Chi transcends the limits of life and death.'

Among a raft of injuries, Raymond had a fractured sternum, indicating his killers probably jumped on his chest as he lay helpless on the ground. The final, fatal blow may have come from a wooden stool found near the body, or a long wooden staff used in karate combat, both of which had been stolen from the back of his car, along with a hiking tent, also missing. Gone were Keam's house and key rings, which contained a picture of his young son, dressed in a blue jumpsuit holding a gold ball. Keam's car, parked about twenty metres away, had been ransacked.

A Department of Main Roads technician, Keam was intending to drive down to Canberra a few days later to join his de facto wife and two-year-old son. On the night of his death, he had trained in the gym at Balmain Leagues Club and had had some dinner at his inner-city Waterloo home. Sometime after midnight he drove his Holden Jackaroo to Alison Park and parked it near the toilet block. Although Keam had been known to frequent gay beats, he didn't identify as homosexual or lead a gay lifestyle.

The subsequent investigation took some curious turns, Page was interested to read. Two weeks after the attack, a handful of soldiers from a crack Army unit trained in hand-to-hand combat offered to help police with an all-night stake-out of Alison Park. They donned civilian clothing and roamed the park while homicide detectives stood on stand-by in the vicinity.

A month later, in response to a report by another man claiming to have been attacked in the park on the same night, police issued descriptions of two men and a woman. The man told police he managed to break free from his attackers and sped off in his car. Police said the woman was about 171 cm tall, with a slight build and waist-length blonde hair, wearing black jeans and a black long-sleeved top. One youth was described as nineteen or twenty years old, 175 cm tall with a solid athletic build, fair complexion and neat collar-length hair. The second was 180 cm tall, with a medium build, black hair and a full beard.

Despite these detailed descriptions, no arrests were made and twelve months later—in January 1988—the state government offered a $50 000 reward for information leading to the arrest of Keam's killers. The inquest in June that year heard how a gang of youths were attacking and robbing gay men in a suburban park. One of the number would lure a victim to a car or secluded spot, where the unfortunate man would be attacked or robbed. Sometimes they would escort him to an automatic teller machine and force him to withdraw money and hand it to them.

The inquest wound up without any specific suspects, however, although the investigation didn't end there. Over eighteen months later, police interviewed members of the gang who had slain Johnson, and some of their mates from Cleveland Street Boys High. But again, no charges were laid.

Maurice McCarty, 53, ballet technician

Murdered at his Linthorpe Street, Newtown, home Sunday April 7, 1991
One man convicted of murder, later acquitted

No-one will probably ever know what Maurice McCarty was discussing with his rough-looking young guest only minutes before he was murdered in his backyard.

McCarty, a solid, unfit man with a thatch of wild grey hair, may have been shooting the breeze about the rugby, one of the few sports he was interested in, or perhaps his work in the ballet, or maybe the joint they were about to share.

All that emerged in court was that he had poured his guest a glass of wine and put on some music. Every now and then the melody of the CD would have been punctuated by the thunder of a passing train from the railway line opposite; and no doubt the cramped living room would have been cooled by the pleasant breeze blowing through the half-open window.

The pair had the house to themselves: McCarty's two flatmates, one of whom was a close friend of some twenty years standing, were out for the night.

McCarty probably imagined he was getting along very well with his guest, which with the help of the wine led him to become overconfident—and make an unwelcome pass.

A bloody, deadly struggle ensued.

Just after 11 p.m. on Sunday April 7, 1991, just as McCarty's neighbours were turning in, they heard moans and cries for help, seemingly from next door's backyard. One of them—a man in his twenties—scaled the fence and found McCarty lying semi-conscious in a pool of blood. He phoned an ambulance and the local Newtown police immediately. Despite emergency treatment at nearby Royal Prince Alfred Hospital, McCarty died early the next day. Police said he was struck once across the back of the head with a wine bottle, repeatedly stabbed with a kitchen knife that lay nearby, and chased into the backyard, where he stumbled on the cement paving before his attacker finished off the assault with a house brick. McCarty's face was battered beyond recognition.

As McCarty lay dying, his killer stole his car keys, ransacked the Victorian semi of jewellery and other personal items, and sped off in his victim's silver Nissan sedan. McCarty's car was later found abandoned in Artarmon with its windscreen smashed. This was later to provide vital evidence in convicting the killer, including the penknife stolen from the victim's body.

A New Zealander, McCarty was only staying in Sydney temporarily, and was due to move back to Melbourne, where he had been living for nearly eleven years, after the ballet season wrapped up. He was last seen around 5 p.m. on that Sunday evening, leaving work at the Sydney Opera House.

A month after the killing, a nineteen-year-old unemployed man, Christopher McKinnon, was charged with his murder, and two others as accessories after the fact. McKinnon claimed in court that McCarty had lured him to his Newtown home with the promise of selling him some cheap marijuana. Instead, he poured him a glass of wine and made a pass.

The sexual overture was too much for McKinnon, who simply 'snapped'. Despite the psychotic nature of the attack, McKinnon claimed in his own defence that he didn't mean to kill McCarty. This didn't stop him leaving his victim in a pool of blood, stealing his car, and boasting to a couple of mates afterwards that he had just 'rolled a fag'.

McKinnon was very persuasive in the dock, expressing his disgust at McCarty's attempt to touch him. His defence team in turn successfully painted McCarty as a sexual predator. Although McKinnon was convicted of murder, he was later acquitted on appeal.

While it may not be a legally recognised term, the 'homosexual panic defence'—the argument that men can be excused of carrying out even horrific violence if it's in response to another man trying to fondle or kiss them—has a long and ignoble tradition in the Australian courts, Sue Thompson had explained to Page during their first meeting.

The strategy worked most effectively when a young, violent offender—without fear of being cross-examined—could express his horror at being drawn into a homosexual act. It appealed to the deep and probably unexpressed homophobia in some juries.

Thompson added that the rules on cross-examination now allow for far more robust questioning of a gay-killer's motives, so the 'homosexual panic defence' is now much trickier for defence teams to pull off. Instead, they tended to go down the path of pleading that the killer had been sexually abused as a child, and suffered a flashback to this early trauma when a gay man propositioned him, thus leading him to an act of uncharacteristic, uncontrolled violence. To juries unaware of a killer's violent or criminal record, this could seem entirely plausible.

Gay hate murders didn't end in 1992, of course—they just occurred less frequently. On Saturday August 22, 1992, the battered and trouserless body of a homosexual middle-aged man, Cyril Olsen, was found floating in Rushcutters Bay. There were no leads and the case was swiftly closed.

Against the backdrop of this horror show of violence, it seemed startling to Page that the police at the time so quickly dismissed John Russell's death and Ross Warren's disappearance as 'accidents'. With so much blood spilled at Bondi, Alexandria and Newtown, how could they regard their deaths as anything but suspicious?

There were many good reasons to treat these as murder investigations from the start. The police already knew that some of the men responsible for other gay murders of the period were serial bashers; how could they rule out the possibility they hadn't killed others? And for that matter, how could they dismiss the scenario that some of the youths responsible for the plague of gay bashings may have graduated to murder?

Maybe the police of the time—Detective Sergeant McCann excepted—simply failed to put the Warren and Russell deaths in a wider context.

So where should he go from here?

Page knew at least some of the answers might be just a short drive away.

7 CASE OF THE MISSING HAIR

Steve Page felt a tight knot form in the base of his stomach. He was standing on the edge of a 12-metre-high cliff at South Bondi, surveying the rock platform below, fixing on the spot where John Russell plunged to his death in the early hours of November 23 1989. As a blustery September wind whipped through his suit, Page clutched tightly to the two crime scene photographs in his left hand, but it took no great effort to pinpoint the spot he was looking for, identified by an unusual wedge-shaped boulder lying nearby. All traces of blood had long since been washed away from the rocky recess where John Russell's body once lay, and the patch of scrub close to where Page was standing, flattened by the victim and his attackers during that brutal encounter, was now upright and thick.

Page had spent his morning with the dead. He had already stopped at the spots on the Bondi cliff tops where Ross Warren had disappeared and a panicked

Kritchikorn Rattanjurathaporn had slipped over the cliff edge trying to flee his attackers. Now, as he stared at the recess in the rock shelf where John landed, shimmering in the spring sunlight because of a gossamer-thin pool of sea water, the last few minutes of the barman's life were flashing through his mind. He could see John in his mind's eye, alone and defenceless in the moonlight, surrounded by a sinister gang of teenagers who would think nothing of crippling him or leaving him for dead. Knowing there was no way out.

Page understood first hand that gut-wrenching feeling of being ambushed. Once, during an undercover operation in Telopea Street, Punchbowl, in Sydney's southwest, then *the* hot spot in the city's Lebanese gang wars, he had been walking a dog past a house where a school boy, Edward Lee, had been stabbed to death in the front yard by a group of youths. The fourteen-year-old had mistaken the address for a birthday party he was to attend. Even though Page was clad in shorts and a T-shirt, one of the suspects, who was reversing out of a driveway, spotted him as a cop and reached for his mobile phone. Within minutes, ten more Middle Eastern youths were streaming out of houses and cars and Page found himself surrounded. This was a standard ploy of gangs like this—to intimidate police by using their mobiles to draw a crowd of mates. 'Hello officer,' one of them sniggered, while another formed a gun with his hand and made pop, pop sounds to the guffaws of the others. The air now thick with tension, Page pushed the call button on his mobile phone so that his partner Al, parked around the corner in an unmarked car, could hear their conversation. He had no sooner shoved one of the smaller youths aside than he could hear the squeal of tires as Al sped into the street. Page made his escape—but not before he was harangued, and they were tailed by three cars.

Page snapped himself out of his dark reverie. He had come here to work out some strategies for his investigation. And to do so, he had to put himself in the mind not just of the victims but of the perpetrators. He looked down at the surf pounding on the rocks. What made this watery killing spot so attractive, he asked himself. Escape would have been paramount, so where would they have run? What was their most direct exit route, he wondered, turning his head towards the apartment blocks towering behind him, and the steps leading up to Marks Park and nearby Fletcher Street.

Where would they have hidden prior to their assaults? The thundering surf may have meant that nothing much was heard by nearby residents; the winding pathway, complete with many nooks in the rock face, provided good hiding spots. Although the pathway was now relatively well lit, back in the late 1980s long stretches of it were cloaked in darkness.

Page climbed the stairs to Marks Park. Although it was mainly a grassy verge—big enough to play a game of football on—parts of it were covered with a camouflage of trees, scrub and hedgerows. In short, a better place to attack someone than a dark laneway. The murderers obviously wanted to leave no witnesses, and from here they could see who came and went.

John Russell's death had rated only a couple of significant mentions in the press, but Warren's disappearance was followed by an avalanche of news stories. There must be someone out there who knows or suspects something—or knows who was responsible.

In the course of his investigation over the next two years, Page would do this coastal walk many times—with bashing victims, who would 'walk' through their assaults, and with witnesses like Craig Ellis, Ross Warren's mate, who pointed to the honeycombed rock face where he found the newsreader's keys, and the spot where his car was parked. When the evidence called for it, Page had an assistant video the scenes.

As beautiful and wild as the headland was, particularly on a sunny day, it was a place that would never cease to haunt Page. It was a place of tragedy.

Page was determined to treat these deaths as if they were fresh homicides. He set about organising door-knocks in all neighbouring apartment blocks, police divers to scour the murky depths around the base of the headland, and for media releases to be sent to the press calling for anyone with information to come forward.

Meanwhile, Page received some bad news from the Crime Scene Unit: it had been unable to locate the hair in John Russell's hand. Or at least, it wasn't where it was supposed to be. When the body was taken to the morgue, all the physical evidence—including those strands of light brown hair—should have been stored in an appropriate container, the details recorded in an exhibit book beside a designated number, and a manila folder filed with the same code. But the box was missing. Page immediately contacted Carl Cameron, a consultant on cold-case homicides, who devoted an entire day searching for the missing evidence. He managed to find the manila folder amongst a batch of others with different numbers. But there was no hair in the folder, or records of what happened to it.

All of which raised the question: did the crime scene detectives called out to John's body on that November morning in 1989 bag the hair? Yes, it would seem so. A check of police records showed that the strands of hair in John's left hand were noted, photographed and bagged. But the constable who so carefully removed the strands of hair from John's hand with plastic gloves and dropped them in a plastic bag was not involved with the investigation after that point. A phone call to the same detective revealed he had no memory of what happened to the exhibits. Nor did the crime scene department at police headquarters have any further explanation. Conveniently for the killer or killers, what Page hoped would be exhibit A had simply vanished.

The missing hair from John Russell's hand, together with his washed clothes, and the fact his body was cremated, put paid to any chance of Page finding some clinching forensic evidence. A blow to his investigation, yes, but hardly a mortal one. There were many other avenues that Page was pursuing, not least the search for new witnesses.

All this meant that those charged with gay bashings between 1988 and 1990 were worth a second look—not to mention those already in prison for the murders of the Thai man and Richard Johnson. Page found that Detective Sergeant Steve McCann, while he was in charge of the investigations into the murders of Rattanajurathaporn and Richard Johnson, had organised about 70 phone taps of the culprits—the so-called Alexandria

Eight—during 1991. These might provide invaluable glimpses into the anti-gay gangs of the time, and provide leads to others.

What Page was hoping to find were some old conversations that could result in some very new leads.

Page asked one of his favourite colleagues, a veteran in transcribing police audio and video interviews, to give him a hand. June was a retirement-age lady with a razor-sharp mind and a quick ear, brilliant at distinguishing muffled words or decoding prison jargon. Page knew that once he had thoroughly briefed June, and advised her of what to look out for, she would be invaluable in highlighting pieces of chat that might be relevant to his investigation.

What Page was ultimately looking for were a few good informers or 'snitches': among those already convicted of gay murders, and among those charged with gay bashings over the same period, there might be one or two who might be willing to spill the beans on their former mates. He knew it would be a frustrating quest. The criminal class—both inside and outside prison—is ruled by a brutal code of silence. Even the toughest thugs are often afraid of what will happen to them if they inform on mates or enemies. So as well as digging up old phone taps, Page set about organising new ones of his own—in prison cells and suburban homes—from his burgeoning 'persons of interest' list.

Of one thing Page was almost certain: he was not dealing with a single serial monster but a multi-headed hydra, a diffuse group of men (and maybe women) who had made it their hobby to kill gays. They were elusive precisely because they were so fragmented. Page had a starting point, however. Killers don't tend to come out of nowhere. In most cases, they have a history—and in this case it would have been bashing gays. Perhaps, having got away with thrashing gay men again and again, they became so emboldened they thought nothing of throwing someone off a cliff. In short, serial bashers who had morphed into serial killers. Or perhaps serial bashers who simply went too far one night.

One mystery continued to nag him, however: what happened to Ross Warren's body? Why hadn't it washed up on Tamarama Beach the next day? Page consulted a lecturer in the School of Geography at the University of NSW whose specialty was coastal geomorphology. Dr Robert Brander was an active member of the Tamarama Surf Club, had snorkelled around Tamarama and Mackenzies Bay, and was familiar with the rock platforms, underwater caves and currents surrounding the headland. He examined synoptic and tidal charts for the Bondi/Tamarama headland for the month of July 1989, and made an estimate of the drift directions on a series of maps. His conclusion: in the 'extremely energetic and turbulent' currents at that time, it was 'highly *unlikely* that any body in the water off the shore platforms, or on the bed [of Tamarama and Bondi] would move landward'. In his accompanying map of drift directions on the Tamarama side of the headland, Brander sketched a number of arrows. They were all pointing *out* towards the Pacific Ocean.

Brander noted an area of intense turbulence around the headland, which is 'why it is often difficult for swimmers and rock fishermen to swim back onto the platform after having fallen off'.

Okay, Page thought, if Warren's body was swept out to sea, why didn't some passing fishing boat see his body floating? He rang Dr Allan Cala, the forensic pathologist, to find out exactly what happens when a body is left floating in the ocean for a few days. A letter he received a few weeks later proved fascinating reading:

> When a deceased body is immersed in the ocean, the body will initially sink. What happens after this depends very greatly on tides and currents, the temperature of the water and the presence of marine creatures and underwater features such as rocks.
>
> After sinking, the body may, but not always, rise to the surface because of decomposition. The buoyancy is created by gas formation and may occur after several days. Clothing may have been stripped off by the forceful action of waves and currents. This explains why some bodies are recovered without clothing.
>
> Bodies do not always rise, and there are instances of persons entering the ocean whose bodies are never recovered.

Page checked the records again. The day after Ross Warren disappeared, the body of another young man was washed up at Dover Heights. It had been floating in the sea for three or four days. This was the unidentified body lying in the morgue on the cold, drizzling Sunday night Craig Ellis was driven there by police, who were trying to determine if it was Ross Warren. But the body, although of a man of Ross's age, clearly wasn't him.

Had this young man, too, been the victim of some horrendous murder? Page checked the records—Clayton Beackon would have gone into the sea two nights before Ross Warren disappeared. On the late afternoon of

Saturday 22 July, 1989, just as Ross Warren's friends were beginning to be concerned that they hadn't heard from him, two spear fishermen were horrified to see a dismembered body floating face down in water about ten metres off shore at Dover Heights.

Police divers, caught up in another retrieval at the time, were unable to recover Beackon's body until the following morning; by early afternoon, it was lying, unidentified, in a freezer drawer at Glebe Morgue; later that night, Craig Ellis and his friend Paul were sitting in the next room ashen-faced, grimly imagining it was Ross Warren.

Clayton Beackon was a good-looking, popular 24-year-old who had trained in the airforce as an electrical tradesman and was known as 'Clay' and 'Cass' to his mates. He was believed to be bisexual and—as Page found—some next of kin were suspicious about the circumstances of his death. Some months after his body was found an anonymous informant contacted Crime Stoppers, claiming that he had drowned near Marks Park. Curiously though, Beackon was known as a strong swimmer.

Page added Beackon's name to his list, but it was only to stay there for a matter of weeks. Sitting in her tidy living room, Beackon's mother told him that her son had left behind what she had always construed to be a suicide note. Tears welling up, she pulled it out of a drawer and handed it to Page:

> Jose, you're my best friend! Wish we could have talked more.
> Clay xxxx
> PS I hope this doesn't happen to Zoey.

When Page returned to the office and checked the coroner's report, he noted that there was as much likelihood that Beackon went into the sea at Diamond Bay—a notorious spot for suiciders—as Bondi.

This was enough for Page to draw a line in the investigative sand. Did Clayton meet with foul play? Yes, it was possible, but the indicators weighed much more heavily on the side of suicide. Nonetheless, Page was struck by the sad coincidence of his going into the ocean only a couple of days before Ross Warren met his fate, and the fact both tragic events occurred against a backdrop of violence and villainy on the Bondi cliff tops.

What stood out so conspicuously was that there was a clear cycle of bodies being recovered—or sighted—off the ocean at the Bondi cliff tops between 1989 and 1990. Page stumbled across another incident report, of two tourists seeing a body floating off the rocks at Mackenzies Point on the Saturday afternoon of December 1, 1990. A subsequent surface and underwater search recovered nothing, however.

The ocean has a way, Page thought, of keeping its secrets.

Sometimes, though, clues get washed up. Page's request for an underwater search around the Bondi headland had turned up something interesting—if not exactly earth-shattering—from the sea floor on the Tamarama side of the headland: a rusted iron water pipe, about a metre long. A perfect instrument for bludgeoning someone, Page thought as he held it up to the light in his office. Which reminded him of something: among the crude tools used in a number of gay bashings around the time of Warren's and Russell's deaths was an iron pipe. He dug up a statement made to police in 1989 by a Robert of Darlinghurst, who had been bashed in Centennial Park with a steel pipe. Tracking down Robert proved simple—he was still at the same address—and the 37-year-old was keen to come to the station.

Page soon found out why. Echoing the feelings of other gay men bashed around this time, who complained that they had been treated shoddily by the police, Robert wanted to spill his bile. It was a sweltering Saturday afternoon just before Christmas 1988, and he had bought some presents from David Jones for a work Christmas party. Walking back home through Centennial Park, and stopping at a dais for a breather and to take in the view, he saw a number of youths attacking a young cyclist near a well-known beat. Robert felt helpless at this point—he was hopelessly outnumbered—but once they had dispersed, he ran over and asked the man whether he was okay. Although battered and bruised, and bleeding from an arm and leg, the man was able, with a bit of assistance from Robert, to get back on his bike.

'Don't you want to report this?' Robert asked him, somewhat dismayed by the victim's nonchalance. 'No, I've had enough for one day,' he said resignedly, setting off.

But when Robert returned to the dais to retrieve his presents, he himself was set upon. One of the seven young toughs used an iron water pipe to smash his elbow and head, but just as he thought he might be a goner, his attackers inexplicably tore off, although not before seizing his wallet and bags. Dazed and bleeding, he stumbled about for ten minutes or so, trying to get his head around what had happened. His short-term memory was affected to the extent that when he returned home, he found it was to a house he had moved out of some months before.

A couple of phone calls, and assistance from friends, helped to get him sorted. But when he brought the police back to the scene of the attack in the early evening, and saw the bloodied iron pipe lying among some long blades of grass, he was amazed—and angry—that the two officers didn't consider the incident serious enough to warrant taking the pipe into evidence. So Robert grabbed it and took himself off to hospital. He had three loose teeth, needed fifteen stitches in his head and later had to have an operation on his elbow.

But Robert wasn't giving up that easily. He returned to the scene of the attack on several occasions, hoping to spot his attackers so he could report them. And then, one Saturday afternoon, bingo! There they were, attacking someone else. Two youths, Michael Kim and Jamie Dempsey, were arrested—as was the rugby league player Darrell Trindall, not for the bashing, but for being troublesome when his mates were taken to the station. However, the courts later dismissed Robert's evidence because the defence successfully argued that he had suffered short-term memory loss, and thus his testimony was unreliable, specifically his identification of his attackers.

Kim and Dempsey walked free. No matter that the two men fitted his initial description to the police to the letter. Perhaps as a bitter memento of how he felt the authorities had let him down, Robert kept the bloodied pipe tucked under his bed for about five years. Alas, during a clean-up three or four years earlier he had finally tossed it out. But Robert was able to describe the pipe as if he still held it in his hands, and its distinctive feature—a shiny tube with a clip at the end—matched that of the one retrieved from the sea bed at Bondi. Did this suggest links between the bashers at Bondi and those prowling Centennial and Moore parks at the same time? Quite possibly, as gay bashers tend not to restrict themselves to just one 'beat'. Still, an iron pipe was hardly clinching evidence.

To determine what connections did or did not exist between the different gay bashings and murders across Sydney, Page started combing through the transcripts of statements made to Detective Sergeant Steve McCann, who in investigating the Johnson and Rattanajurathaporn murders, had smartly cast his net to see if those charged and convicted had been guilty of other earlier offences.

Page came across a sworn statement to police, from a youth worker at Keelong Detention Centre back in March 1991 who heard the following conversation between Adam French, then serving a sentence for the manslaughter of Richard Johnson, and a pair of other inmates while they were eating lunch. The topic at the large communal table was homosexuality. She recalled the following exchange:

'I pushed a poofter off the cliff at Bondi,' said Adam French. 'I hate poofters.'

'What, into the water?' his mate MB asked.

'Na, onto the fucking rocks,' said French.

After several interruptions and a further question from one of his lunch mates, French mentioned that he 'had walked out onto the rocks and threw this poof's keys into the ocean. He was really pissed off and a fight, scuffle and yelling match started.'

When police questioned French about these statements two weeks later—and queried him about the murders at Bondi—he pleaded ignorance and denied any involvement.

The youth worker, however, was undeterred. In a quiet moment some days later she again asked French if he knew anything. At first he declared no. But after she persisted with, 'Are you sure? Which murder were they [the police] talking about? There were five or six, weren't there?' French replied, 'Yeah, you know the poof that was killed a year before I was arrested.'

'Are you sure?'

'Yeah I know, but I'm not telling.'

Some days later, the youth worker raised the same subject again with French.

'Adam, you know what we were talking about the other night?'

'Yeah,' following a long pause.

'Well I spoke to a friend of mine who is a detective and I sort of gave him some details, but no names, and he said if you gave useful information, you could probably get a reduction in your sentence.'

'I can't.'

'But you didn't have anything to do with it, so you could . . .'

'No, I don't want to anyway.'

◆

Meanwhile, June's sleuthing through the 1991 phone taps organised by Sergeant McCann turned up this disturbing exchange between French and his former

Cleveland Street school mate Dean Howard (also in prison for the murder of Johnson).

'Bondi, man that was like Moore Park. You know the walkway that goes around ... when you go from Bondi to Tamarama ... There's all fuckin' tunnels, mate, and it leads up in the bushes ... There's all poofters up in there, heaps of them ... I don't know who was there, man, but they hit him with this skateboard ... Cracked him ... He just fuckin' screamed like they all do. "Oh, let me go." Just kept crackin' him. Someone pushed him over the thing about, like three- or four-foot drop, something like that.'

At this point Howard interjected: 'Who pushed him, you?'

French: 'No, not me. I was going over to pick up his skateboard, I was gunna hit him again. "Ah help, help." Heaps funny. Used to love how they scream.'

Howard: 'What did you say when you first seen him?'

'Oh, well, I wasn't, I wasn't there when they said something to him first off,' replied French. 'I was comin' down from the top, from where the lookout is. One of the boys said, "You're a poof, eh." And I've come running down the stairs, and I just looked around, mate. They were punchin' into him.'

'Who was that?' Howard asked.

'Kerry, Justin, Manuel, James, who else was there? I think little Popey was down too, Justin Pope. They beat him, fuckin' grabbed his keys, ran back up the car, searched his car ... I think it was a Camry ... three keys—front door key and two car keys. Just went down there, couldn't find nothing in the car, found about $3. "See these, c***?" Just tossed them ... in the sea ...

we've done a bolt, left him, went around to Tama, caught the bus home.'

A bashing on the cliff tops. Keys tossed over the edge. Didn't this sound suspiciously like the disappearance of Ross Warren? Page didn't believe so. Warren's keys were found not in the ocean but on a rock ledge, there were eight keys not three, his car wasn't a Camry, nor did it show any signs of being searched. French went on to describe their victim as a 'pretty big' lad—hardly a description that matched Warren—and French went on to say the attack happened 'about eleven, eleven-thirty', hours before Warren disappeared. The boys got a bus home, suggesting a pre-midnight departure.

But there was something even more fundamental. The victim, whoever it was, appeared to have survived. He stood up on the rock ledge below and was screaming as they left him. So who was this man? Page crosschecked other records of gay bashings on the cliff tops and could find nothing that matched it exactly. Translation: whoever was bashed on that day chose not to go to police, or if he did, the records had been lost.

What this tape brought home, however, was that some members of the Alexandria Eight were bashing gay men in other parts of Sydney, including Bondi. French admitted in subsequent police statements to bashing hundreds of gay men, including at Bondi, but denied killing anyone there. In a bugged conversation from July 7, 1991, which was later admitted to the inquest, he boasted:

> We went to Centennial, eh. You were there when we got the guy with the wig . . . There was Trindall, me, Sharkey and Brad. We were just gonna walk by him and Sharkey

goes, 'I know that poofter, man. I've seen him before, I've belted him before.' They'd belted him at Moore Park, when they was up the Cross before and took his wig. Trindall pissed in it and they chucked it in a hollow tree. Just knockin' him around, man, slapped on the ... that was one of the funniest days, man.

Page could still recall the statements of the presiding judge in the Johnson murder, contained in the transcripts from the court case. In sentencing the eight young men he said he believed they were genuinely remorseful and unlikely to offend again. But these didn't sound like the words of remorseful, guilt-stricken young men. For them, the bashings and deaths were all just a game.

In another tape, French claimed that Ronald Morgan—also a member of the Alexandria Eight who slew Richard Johnson—and another youth, Norm Kassas, were involved in bashing gay men at Tamarama on an 'almost daily' basis.

Page ascertained that the Trindall in question was Darrell Trindall, former rugby league footballer, first for the South Sydney Rabbitohs, and later the Canterbury Bulldogs. Trindall and French had been mates at school and had played footy together. While the bugged conversations didn't mean they were murder suspects, it certainly qualified them as persons of interest.

Then there was the statement from a former NSW constable, Sarah O'Brien, who lived in Wollongong in the late 1980s. She recalled a troubling conversation with her flatmate's friend, a woman called Merlyn McGrath, in August 1989, who claimed she went 'poofter bashing' with male friends. Constable O'Brien asked her why she did this and McGrath replied, 'to teach them a lesson not to be f*** poofters.' Then she went on to tell Constable O'Brien that one of them was 'the bloke off TV . . . that Warren fella' and that she feared he might be dead because he had been thrown off a cliff. She said they rolled him and bashed him and threw him over some cliff.

Constable O'Brien's flatmate, and her flatmate's mother, also recalled the conversation, although the former thought it might have been later, in April 1991, while the mother recalled it some weeks after the Warren disappearance. When McGrath was contacted by police at the time, she denied the accounts. Page set about contacting all the people mentioned in the statement again.

Another person he was keen to track down was a jogger called Rod, who regularly ran between Tamarama and Bondi during the late 1980s, and who made a statement to police in December 1989 following the death of John Russell. Rod believed he had spoken to someone who had been on the cliff-top walk the night John Russell was thrown over. Page invited him into the station for an interview. Many years might have elapsed but, as he found, Rod remembered that period of his life as if it were yesterday:

> Occasionally I would hang around in the hope that I might meet someone for casual sex. So in '89 I met up with this chap who I called Red because of his henna-red hair. He was someone, a gay man, who went to the rocks area pretty regularly. So I'd just pass the time of day with him and ask him, what's been happening, just to get a bit of an idea if there'd been any trouble. I'd been assaulted myself in 1986, so I guess the subject was of interest to

me. 'Red' showed me knife scars on his upper body from when he'd been assaulted but managed to fight them off. Anyway at the end of '89 he mentioned that he had heard sounds of a bashing, but it was windy and he couldn't hear very well. So I just accepted that for what it was worth, and then coincidentally, probably about two or three weeks later, someone I knew came to visit me from the country. He said that a friend of his, John Russell, had been found dead at the bottom of a cliff at Bondi.

I wasn't there when John Russell went over, I wasn't there on the night that Red heard what might have been a bashing. I just felt that I should go to the police station. At the sergeant's suggestion I raised the subject again with Red when I saw him again in early 1990. I asked him for more details and he said there were a number of voices, but he couldn't make out clearly what was being yelled. He said the shouting came from the northern side of the peninsula and he was on the southern side or up on the park somewhere.

And I said, look, there's a possibility a death happened that night and it was John Russell. I suggested he make a statement to the police and offered to drive him to the station. But he made it clear he wasn't interested in talking to the police. After I spoke to him that second time, I returned to the station and the officer—a Sergeant Ingleby—said he would come to the Bondi rocks to have a look for Red. I think I suggested a Sunday night because that's usually the busiest night at the rocks. Ingleby put his running gear on and we walked all around, and although a few gay men were around, Red wasn't there.

Rod only saw the mysterious Red one more time—about a month later in the distance—and he swiftly disappeared. All that Rod knew about him was that he had a twin brother in the Navy. Why was Red so reluctant to take his information to the police? Rod could only speculate to Page's associate Constable Bernadette Ingram:

> Red seemed like he could handle himself; I imagine he was pretty handy with his fists. He was of working-class origin, I'd say, as I am. He might have been known to the police in some way. He didn't seem to have a job, for example . . .

The deaths at Bondi clearly had a big effect on Rod at the time. He told Constable Ingram that after the murder of Kritchikorn Rattanajurathaporn he went around to gay pubs and gay community centres putting up posters, asking anyone with further information on the killing to contact the police.

Meanwhile, Page's assistants were well advanced in a wave of cold-calling friends and former colleagues of Warren and Russell. Unfortunately, with the passage of time and the scourge of AIDS, some had passed away; others were living overseas, and some weren't interested in dredging up unhappy memories. Page was facing an increasingly uphill battle to get new witnesses to come forward—to do that, he would need to draw public attention to the case. He had already been talking to his contacts in the media, and stories were beginning to appear in *The Sydney Morning Herald* and *The Daily Telegraph*. But Page wanted more: he wanted prime-time TV. He had a meeting with colleagues and searched around for an idea for weeks.

◆

The idea hit him while he was driving to work one morning. He was mulling over the position of John's body and how to prove he must have been pushed rather than a victim of a drunken fall. The only way was a re-enactment—so why not make it a media-friendly re-enactment, one that would create a buzz on the evening news and morning papers?

But first, he needed a dummy—and no ordinary dummy. One that would not only match John's approximate shape and weight, but one that was also realistic enough to look human in a fall and catch the eye of the media. A typical shop dummy would be too light and rigid for his purposes, and one kindly offered to him by the fire brigade, which could be filled up with sand to the weight required, proved to be too formless. Somewhat at a loss, he contacted a friend who was a set designer in the film industry, who pointed him to a warehouse in Sydney's Fox studios. Amid the sea of dummies, Page chose one that most closely matched John's size and height. It had already been a star in the acclaimed Australian film *Lantana*, and if everything worked to plan Page would make it a star on the evening news. The film's producers kindly agreed to donate it.

Page chose a Sunday morning to stage his re-enactment—first because crowds of people would be there doing the popular cliff walk, and second because this is traditionally the 'softest' news day of the week—the best time to attract journalists hungry for a decent story. Via the police department's media section, he sent out a barrage of invitations to newspapers and television stations across the city.

The idea worked brilliantly. As a small crowd of curious onlookers stood nearby, a constable from the Police Rescue and Bomb Unit pushed the 55 kg dummy—the weight of John Russell—off the twelve-metre cliff at the exact spot where John was pushed over. The exercise was repeated six times—face first, back first—while television cameras purred away and journalists scribbled in their notebooks.

Page explained to the press what they were hoping to achieve. 'I need witnesses who were either present or saw John Russell or Ross Warren meet their demise to come forward and assist us,' he told reporters. 'A lot of the crimes passed off as isolated suicides or disappearances at that time were in fact gay hate crimes.'

When asked by one reporter what a 'hate crime' was, Page replied: 'When someone is killed to make a point. The twisted belief that gays—or blacks or Asians, pick your scapegoat—don't deserve to live. Hate crimes aren't about money—although they can involve robbery—or jealous rage. They're about cold calculation and frenzied violence. Back in the '70s and '80s, poofter bashing was a sport.' A pause. 'A blood sport.'

Another journalist asked whether Page believed the perpetrators of the Russell murder may have been responsible for others. 'I've come to the conclusion that there was a series of gangs, and to some degree there were crossovers between them. They wouldn't just hit one beat, they'd travel around until they were cashed up sufficiently to satisfy their needs and then move on.'

Detective Inspector Terry Dalton spoke to the cameras: 'I would urge any members of the community who may have been assaulted and not reported it to the police to make contact through Paddington Police Station.'

Page's experiment confirmed that it would have been highly unlikely that John would have been able to twist his body around if he had fallen off the cliff accidentally, or even of his own volition. Page's greater ambition, however, was for the re-enactment to draw publicity, and in this the gamble hit pay dirt. In the following days, the switchboard at Paddington Police Station often lit up with callers wanting to relate their own horrendous stories. A handful later came into the station to give statements about bashings and their near-death experiences, not only at the Bondi cliff tops but other beats across Sydney in the late 1980s and early 1990s.

But there was one man who stood out. A man who had narrowly escaped with his life after being brutally bashed and dragged to the very cliff edge. A man who had stared death in the eye for ten terrifying minutes—at the same spot John Russell was thrown over. Barely a month after the Bondi barman was killed.

Page thought he might have the ultimate witness.

The man who got away.

8 THE MAN WHO GOT AWAY

'Throw the poofter off! Throw him off!' bellowed the crazed teenagers, as the ringleader—a slim, tallish youth with cropped fair hair and an icy glare in his blueish eyes—dragged his victim along the concrete pathway to a peak on the cliff face high enough to mean certain death if you fell.

'Rick', a 22-year-old waiter at a Bondi cafe, had been out for a routine run on that hot summer night, Thursday December 21, 1989, almost a month to the day after John Russell was pushed to his death.

As the wiry, doe-eyed young man lay alone and defenceless at the mercy of these young thugs, the ringleader barked the words that would stay with him for years to come: 'Let's throw him off where we threw the other one off . . .'

◆

Only hours before, as the sun slid behind the mismatched pastel quilt that is the Bondi skyline, Rick had walked home from his job as a waiter on Campbell Parade to his apartment no more than two minutes walk away, tossing up whether to go for a run that night. Although the heat of the late afternoon had eased off a few degrees, it was still unseasonably warm for this time of year. He would leave his run until much later, he decided, until well after dinner, when the tourists would be gone from the cliff tops, when Marks Park would be almost deserted.

Except for the men who went there to socialise and cruise for sex, that is.

Rick knew what went on there—he'd been to the cliff tops several times before—and had even hooked up with a couple of young men who he'd invited back to his tiny one-bedroom flat. One had even become a friend. Truth be told, he found a run or stroll around these cliff tops so much easier than fronting up to one of Oxford Street's gay bars. That first step into the darkness of a bar or club was always so intimidating. The hungry eyes checking you out. The attitude—real or imagined—from the good-looking ones. The preening gym bunnies. The leather queens. He always had to gird himself for those first five or ten minutes. Only after the warm glow of those first couple of beers sank in could he start to relax and enjoy himself.

Not that the cliff tops were necessarily a sanctuary from anxiety or apprehension either. He'd never encountered any trouble there, but he'd heard enough stories to make him watchful and wary. Still, after a tough day at the cafe, when a long and lonely evening stretched out ahead of him, a run to the cliff tops seemed as good a distraction as any. It seemed safe enough.

So as the clock on his kitchen wall ticked towards 10.30 p.m., Rick pulled on his jogging shorts, sneakers and singlet. He decided to run the full length of the beach promenade tonight, first to the Ben Buckler headland in North Bondi, before turning back and making the ascent up Notts Avenue on the more rocky southern headland. Jogging past the famous Bondi Icebergs swimming club and pool he slowed down a little to catch his breath and wipe his brow. It struck him how strangely quiet it was for such a clear moonlit night.

Scaling a flight of stairs at Marks Park, however, the mood and scene suddenly shifted. He was face to face with a group of about a dozen teens aged between fifteen and twenty, most of them perched on a stone wall lining the pathway.

'What are you doin' here?' one teenager barked at him, before demanding money and cigarettes.

'You're a poofter, aren't you?' spat another, stepping forward and glaring at him menacingly.

Somehow, Rick managed to evade this bunch of hoons by continuing to push forward. He didn't stop running for the next half hour or so, skirting the circular lookout area of Mackenzies Point—where not a soul was to be seen—and around to Tamarama before doubling back on the same winding pathway towards home. The encounter with the louts had been unnerving, but he imagined they would have scurried off by now. Certainly the pathway ahead looked reassuringly clear.

Rick was only about six or seven metres from the last set of stairs towards Notts Avenue when suddenly a figure jumped out of the shadows and knocked him onto the grass. Once he was down he was set upon by four or five others who repeatedly kicked and punched him. He looked up to see the ringleader's boot directly above his head, ready to stomp him. His right temple felt the full force of its heel.

'What are you?' the ringleader barked, now belting Rick in the ribs repeatedly. 'You're a poofter, aren't you?'

Someone seized Rick's left foot and tried to dislocate it.

'What are you, c * * *?' the ringleader repeated.

'I'm a homosexual,' Rick cried, now doubled up in agony, although his voice was drowned out by the guffaws of his attackers.

While he copped blow after blow, had his earring torn out of his ear lobe and his signet ring ripped from his finger, Rick gave out some vein-popping screams. If anything, this seemed to enrage the ringleader even more.

'You're a poofter and you don't deserve to live,' he snarled, as the group chanted 'gay, gay, gay'.

One of his attackers, wielding a large stick, joked to the others that he would use it to sexually assault him.

What burned into Rick's memory most, however, were the two girls, laughing and goading on the boys to thump harder. And the whites of their eyes. High on hatred.

Rick shuddered at the memory. 'Still to this day,' he told Steve Page, 'it runs through my mind, how they stood by and laughed while the others beat into me.' The pair were standing on the pathway on the southern side of the headland, looking back towards the Bondi skyline.

With the help of another detective and a video-camera operator, Page was doing a 'walk around' of the crime scene with Rick, who had guided them along the exact route of his run on that awful night.

Rick stared silently out to sea for a moment or two. 'How could those girls do that?' he asked.

All too easily, it seemed to Page. Group dynamics—peer pressure in its most ghastly form—can quickly turn a straggly crowd into a bloodthirsty mob, he explained to Rick. He'd seen aspects of it before in everything from bar-room brawls to crowd control. When a ringleader or authority figure eggs on those around him to behave sadistically, the group soaks up the power and bloodlust. It comes back to one human being, or a group of human beings, enjoying complete control over another.

Rick had become their plaything and they were free to torment him at will. They clearly took pleasure from it.

As they strolled around the winding pathway on this mellow August afternoon in 2001, Rick and Page had plenty of time to talk.

'I haven't been back here since it happened,' Rick reflected.

'At the time you knew it was a gay beat—and dangerous?' Page asked.

'Yeah.'

'Then why did you run here at this time of night?'

'Because you never think it will happen to you.'

The face of the ringleader was firmly imprinted in his mind. He estimated the attack lasted about fifteen to twenty minutes. 'But when you're in the thick of being bashed like that, ten seconds can seem like an eternity,' he admitted. 'One attacker said, "Don't let him look at us, he knows me" and pulled his black sloppy joe over his head so I couldn't see,' he recalled. 'Then the ringleader pushed my face into the ground and started to drag me around. I remember trying to protect my face because I had an interview the following week. It's funny what you think of at the time.'

Survival, rather than a bruised face or black eye, was soon the only thing on Rick's mind after the ringleader dragged him by the shoulders towards the precipice, ably assisted by one of his mates. That's when Rick kept hearing those terrifying words, repeated two or three times:

'I'm gonna throw you over the side.'

They dragged him down three flights of stairs, past at least half-a-dozen blocks of home units—nearly 500 metres—towards the cliff edge. Remarkably, no-one heard his cries for help, or if they did chose to ignore them. The only person brave enough to deal with this vicious onslaught was Rick himself.

'I had to think fast,' he said. And so he did: after violently elbowing one of his two principal attackers, who yelped with pain, there was a moment's eerie silence, a sudden meltdown in the melee.

Rick saw his chance. Catching a glimpse of a fragment of staircase through a break in the group, and charged on adrenaline, he flew up the stairs to nearby Fletcher Street, before catching sight of a light switching on in an apartment. Someone must have heard something. Rescue at last.

Rick looked up beseechingly at the twentysomething man now standing on his balcony. He yelled out that he'd been bashed.

'I'm not going to help you,' the man shouted back. 'I don't help poofters.'

Then nothing. The light went out.

Blood trickling from one ear, with swollen eyes, four loose teeth, a fractured finger, and no shoes, Rick continued his frantic flight up Fletcher Street, before daring to look back to see if his assailants were still behind him.

A deep, exquisite breath of relief. They had given up the chase.

He stumbled back to his apartment in Campbell Parade, the tears spilling down his bruised cheeks. For the first few minutes after closing the front door behind him he simply sat down, stared into space, and with his arms folded, swayed from side to side in shock. Then, with trembling hands, he called a close friend. And then, the Bondi Police.

Two detectives were at his house within 45 minutes, but there was little they could do at this point, they said. A friend drove him to the emergency department of the Prince of Wales Hospital, where at 1.30 a.m. he received treatment for concussion and a raft of other injuries. Just as dawn was breaking over Bondi, he put his key in the door and collapsed in bed.

A week afterwards, he dutifully strode into Bondi Police Station to make a comprehensive, four-page statement. But he didn't hear back from them until months later.

As the video camera whirred away, and the other detective jotted something in his notebook, Page and Rick stood on the approximate spot on the precipice where he was dragged. 'This,' said Rick, 'is where they tried to push me off.'

Page knew this spot very well. Looking down the face towards a now familiar boulder lying on the rock platform below, and down the pathway ahead of him, he was standing about 10 metres from where John Russell had been hurled to his death eleven years before. A lone council seat now marked the spot. Page and his would-be star witness sat down on the seat.

Lighting up a cigarette, Rick recalled that for months after the attack, he was nervous about going out alone, especially at night. 'Not just because of the events of that night,' he said, 'but because a few weeks later the main guys who attacked me walked past the cafe where I worked, and then I saw them further down the street one day.' That cafe, he explained, was adjacent to a surf shop and arcade popular with many local youths.

'So I assumed they were locals, maybe had seen me before, and that's why one of them didn't want me to see his face. And of course, that meant, for all I knew, they could have been living across the street from me.'

The words, 'Don't let him look at us, he knows me' thus had a terrible resonance for a long time afterwards, he explained.

About six months after the attack, two detectives from the homicide squad came to the cafe where Rick worked to show him a number of photographs. And there, staring right back at him, was the face of his principal attacker, only with a slightly different haircut. The next day Rick went off to Waverley Police Station for formal identification, signing and dating photograph number eleven. He picked out Sean Cushman—who was well known to police at the time—and claimed he was the ringleader, the one who yelled at him:

'Let's throw him off where we threw the other one off...'

Was Rick certain the man in the photo was Sean Cushman?

'When I first made a statement to police a few days after the attack, I wanted to be sure I identified the right guy, and not incriminate someone who was innocent,' Rick explained. 'But after I saw my attacker again in the street in the months following the attack, I was very confident it was the guy in the photograph I signed.'

Rick didn't hear from the detectives again. By the end of 1990 he decided he'd had enough of Bondi, quit his job and moved closer to the city. Time inevitably marched on. Rick moved overseas for some years. He got a job in London, travelled through Europe, fell in love, fell out of love. In 1999, feeling homesick and wanting to settle down, he returned to Sydney.

As Rick continued to drag on his cigarette, Page listened intently. 'Those teenagers who tried to kill me—they'd be approaching 30 now,' he said quietly. 'They're still out there—somewhere.'

Where might they be, Rick wondered. And what about the two women who laughed while his ribs were being crushed and his head reduced to a pulp? Do they ever think back to the times when they went out with their boyfriends bashing and even killing? Do they have children now? As they're tucking their kids in at night, do they think about what they once did?

Rick drew hard on his cigarette. He promised Page he would testify at an upcoming inquest, but only if his real name was suppressed. After stabbing out his cigarette butt on the side of the bench he looked around sheepishly—there was no bin for him to drop his cigarette into and he didn't want to flick the butt into the scrub. Not in front of a policeman.

◆

Later that afternoon, after Rick had made his statement, Page dug up Rick's initial police statement, dated January 1990. Attached to it was a report filed by the constable in charge at the time:

> From information received from [Rick's real name here] I am aware that assaults and robberies of homosexuals is a popular pastime with the juvenile and hoodlum element, unfortunately most of the victims who are homosexual do not report the incidents to police when they occur as they may not want publicity. I believe that the level of 'unreported' assaults and associated offences on the homosexual element in this area (and other areas) would be extremely high.

At least, Page thought, some recognition of the real extent of the gay-bashing problem on the cliff tops. But this recognition wasn't carried any further than a few paragraphs in this report. And the phrase 'popular pastime with the juvenile element' had an air of trivialising the violence, as if this were just another numbingly routine problem. There was no mention of the death of John Russell, which occurred only a few weeks before, and the disappearance of Ross Warren only a few months earlier. Most alarming of all, there was no suggestion that the violence could be stopped or slowed with some practical policing—perhaps an officer or two to patrol the cliff tops, perhaps an all points bulletin to other officers to keep a lookout for trouble in the area, perhaps some public-interest warnings in outlets such as the local papers.

And so the assaults continued, with increasing brazenness, with increasing ferocity. Calls to anti-violence lines were skyrocketing, and the gay community was turning out in its hundreds in front of State Parliament to demonstrate against the violence. But neither politicians, police, nor Crown prosecutors seemed able to stem the rising tide of attacks.

When Page typed Cushman's name into a police records system he found a long string of offences, but it was a particular period he was interested in. Between March 28, 1987 and May 1, 1992, he found that Cushman had come under the notice of the police 32 times for offences ranging from driving in a dangerous manner, stealing, possessing a prohibited drug and wilfully marking walls, to the far graver charges of violent disorder and assault. Besides the attack on Rick, two others during this period stood out. On Sunday November 12, 1989, Cushman was charged—along with two others—for a brutal attack on a man after an outdoor concert in Bondi.

◆

'C'mon fellows, let a bloke through,' Robert T requested of the teenagers blocking the pathway behind the Bondi Pavilion, many milling around a ghetto-blaster. One, a thick-set Pacific Islander with a maroon and yellow cap, sipping from a stubbie of VB, stepped in front of him, refusing to let him pass, while his mate, wearing an American Navy baseball cap, stretched the branch of a small tree in front of him. After Robert tried to sidestep the group by walking onto the grass, the youth in the American Navy cap let the branch go, whacking him in the back, while another teenager in a lumber-jacket jostled him.

As Robert strode swiftly away, members of the group hurled a couple of empties at him and yelled abuse. One youth tossed himself in the air and walloped Robert in the chest with a karate kick, which caused him to fall. The youth in the American Navy cap then laid into him with punches and kicks.

'Why don't you fight, ya cunt?' he bawled.

After taking punches and kicks from five or six youths—Robert compared it to being like 'under a tin roof in heavy rain'—he heard a burly mate of his yelling, 'get off him, get off him', whereupon the youths swiftly retreated. Reduced to a bloody mess, Robert nonetheless made it to Bondi Police Station, which despatched five police officers to the rear of the Bondi Pavilion. Robert pointed out his three principal attackers—the Pacific Islander, the youth in the lumber-jacket and the one wearing an American Navy cap, identified by police as Sean Leigh Cushman.

◆

Just over a month later, Cushman was arrested with two others for an even more savage bashing near Marks Park. Alan B had parked his car in Notts Avenue, went to Bondi surf club to meet a few mates, and returned to his car to find it wouldn't start. While checking under the bonnet, he was suddenly set upon by three young men who shoved him to the ground and started kicking him.

Alan managed to get to his feet and run a short distance before being caught again. One of them barked, 'Are you gay?' before laying into him and seizing his wallet and car keys. The three then searched his car and tossed his keys into the ocean. Before they tore off, however, they struck Alan in the chest with a skateboard. He collapsed holding his chest, moaning in agony. With the help of one of his mates, he later sought treatment at St George Hospital in Sydney's south, where he lived.

Alan—like Robert T, a heterosexual—later identified Sean Cushman and David McAuliffe as his attackers, but they were never charged with this offence. Only seven months later, McAuliffe—with the help of his brother Sean and mate Matthew Davis—would go on to slaughter the gentle Thai waiter, Kritchikorn Rattanjurathaporn, whose horribly battered body would be found trapped in an underwater ledge.

◆

Page fished through Steve McCann's old reports and found the following, dated April 1991:

> Cushman is reputedly the leader of a loosely connected gang of street thugs who have been terrorising people in the Bondi Beach and south Bondi area for some considerable time. Cushman has yet to be interviewed for his part in a gang attack on [Rick's real name] on 21 December 1989. In that instance Cushman with other offenders

assaulted and robbed [Rick], and threatened to throw him off the cliff.

Page had already established that the gang McCann referred to was the Bondi Boys. He'd contacted a few police officers working in Bondi at the time, who recalled this gang of street fighters and graffiti artists with particular disdain. Cushman seemed to be their leader, mentor and goad. One of the officers, in an intelligence report submitted on September 30, 1989, had noted that when Cushman and four other members of the gang were searched for a potential street crime, one of them was found to have a piece of paper in his pocket with the words 'Bondi Boys' scrawled across it, and the letters 'PTK' underneath.

PTK or People That Kill was the menacing tag used by gang members to credit their spray-painted colour designs on buildings around Bondi. Most members of the Bondi Boys had been charged with bashing and robbery offences, including Cushman's best mate Timothy Alger. But it wasn't just old police reports that pointed to Cushman as the head of the Bondi Boys. Three other witnesses whom Page tracked down claimed Cushman was their leader.

One witness, Tobias R, who was at Dover Heights High School at the same time as Cushman, and whose sister was friendly with a couple of the Bondi Boys, claimed that all their teenage peers knew Marks Park was a gay beat. Gang members Cushman and Ned Hadjukovic wanted 'to pick on the gay people' because they hated them. Tobias said that the Bondi Boys used two graffiti tags: PTK and PSK (Park Side Killers).

He remembered seeing the tag spray-painted around Bondi at the time, especially on the walls and rock faces of the cliff-side walk between Bondi and Tamarama. (Interestingly, Page noted, Cushman had been pulled up by the police for disfiguring public property in 1988.)

Tobias claimed that Sean and Ned would often brag about 'bashing and robbing poofters' and recalled one instance in the summer of 1989 when they returned from the park with spots of blood on their clothes and hands.

Cushman was now under Page's spotlight, and he set his detectives on to finding out the names of all those who were in Cushman's immediate orbit in the late 1980s and early 90s.

In short, he wanted the definitive list of the Bondi Boys.

Still, Cushman was only one of about 30 'persons of interest' that he had now netted—all involved in assaults around Bondi at the time Warren and Russell died. Some of these names, he noticed, were subsequently charged with other criminal enterprises, mostly drug trafficking.

Page knew that Rick's miraculous escape—and his forthcoming testimony—would make him a star witness at the new inquest into the deaths of Russell and Warren. He'd already had a meeting with the coroner, Jacqueline Milledge, at the Glebe Coroner's Court, in which he'd presented an honest and unvarnished summary of his investigation so far. He found her not only attentive, but also supportive, seeming to prize the evidence he was marshalling together.

◆

Only a few weeks earlier, amid all the 'investigative noise' created by the re-enactment of John Russell's fall off the cliff face—new witnesses coming forward, new statements being made—Page had learned to his surprise that the barbarism on the cliff tops wasn't limited to bashings and murder. When he rang up one bashing victim, who had reported being knocked to the ground near his home in Carlisle Street, Bondi, in January 1990 after withdrawing his $150 rent money from an automatic teller machine, Page found himself listening to the man relay the details of another far more serious and bizarre attack. The victim—a 47-year-old Wollongong resident called Craig Jones—described how he had been raped on the cliff tops by three men 'only a few weeks before Mardi Gras', in March 1990.

'It was traumatic, but I was too ashamed to go to the police, and I wasn't confident they'd be interested anyway,' Jones lamented. He said he was sitting on a council seat in Marks Park at around 1 a.m. when he was approached by a white, tattooed man in his early twenties who invited him into the bushes for sex, where he was ambushed by two others.

'It was only six months or so after my friend Ross Warren disappeared there.'

It sounded like this man had something to offer the investigation.

The next morning, Page and one of his constables, picked up Jones—a sparrow of a man with thinning grey hair and a raspy voice—from Central Station, after he had disembarked from Wollongong. Their passenger appeared anxious, his eyes darting about like some small, scurrying animal. But he did like to talk. Sydney, he explained, made him nervous: he rarely came up to the city these days. 'A lot of water under the bridge.'

Half an hour later the trio were standing at the base of the cliffs on the Tamarama side of Marks Park, peering into a honeycombed pocket of rock. 'This was where Ross Warren's keys were found,' Page explained to Jones, who now seemed more relaxed.

'Someone would have lured Ross down here,' Jones told the two policemen with conviction. 'He would have followed, or accompanied them down the stairs. I don't believe he would have come down here by himself in the pitch dark. He probably put his keys onto this ledge so he could collect them when he was finished. Some men used to come down here for privacy—to get away from the track, where no-one can see you from the top.'

While Jones's theory was interesting and certainly plausible, Page wasn't sold on it. Supposing that Ross *did* descend the stairs and drop the keys onto the rock ledge for safekeeping as Jones surmised—and why would he bother doing that if he was now face to face with his attackers?—it didn't gel on one vital point. The keys would have been seen by the killer or killers, who would have used them to open Ross's car, rifle through it and seize valuables. But there was no indication that the car had been opened at all. Ross's valuables, including his wallet, were untouched.

A more likely scenario was that the keys had been thrown off the cliffs by the killers, in line with other bashings of the time, and that perhaps an angler or beachcomber had spotted them lying on a rock, picked them up and left them in an easy-to-see location nearby for the owner if he or she came back. There had, after all, been more than a two-day gap between Ross's disappearance and Craig Ellis discovering the car keys on the ledge. And scores of people would have been clambering over the rocks in the course of a busy weekend. And of course, as intriguing a clue as the keys were, they provided no foolproof locator of where Ross went over, as the killer may have run along a lengthy section of the path before tossing them over.

Jones first came to Marks Park, he explained, as a twelve-year-old in 1966, and got to know the Bondi and Tamarama areas really well as a teenager. It has been a gay beat, he said, for generations. 'But a lot of people thought the beat at Marks Park was the small toilet block on the Tamarama side; this wasn't really the case. The toilets are too open and people can always walk in on you.' Rather, it was the rocky area on the perimeter of Marks Park and the bushes on top of the flat area of the park that were the favoured cruising spots because they were so private, Jones added. 'When I lived in Bondi I came here nearly every night, but not necessarily for sex. Sometimes just for company.'

Scaling the stairs back to the top of the cliffs, Jones recalled the media circus surrounding Ross's disappearance. 'Newspaper stories and the TV said that he had gone missing or committed suicide. But the rumour in the gay community was that he was murdered and his body dumped off the rocks here.'

Jones, who at the time of Ross's disappearance lived just around the corner in Carlisle Street, added that Bondi had a dark underbelly of street crime in those days. 'It was particularly dangerous if you were gay.'

Jones was leading the two men to the approximate

spot on the cliff tops where he had been attacked. 'It was pool-competition night at the Bondi Hotel—a Friday—and I probably had about four full-strength schooners,' he explained. 'It was hot and I was wearing black nylon cycle shorts and a singlet, with my long blond hair falling down to the middle of my back,' he added, half laughing at himself at the memory. 'I left the pub around 12.30 a.m.'

The then 35-year-old, who was a featherweight 46 kg at the time, and at only 160 cm tall was an easy target, decided to walk home via Marks Park, stopping at a council seat overlooking the ocean to 'watch the moon rise'. After a few minutes a man in his early twenties with dark hair and a light cotton shirt sat next to him and asked him for a light. 'As I lit his cigarette he grabbed my hand and put it on his crotch. At this point I realised I was "on", that he was there to have sex.

'He then led me down the hill and off the footpath into some bushes. He pulled down his jeans and underwear around his ankles, exposing his penis. I voluntarily performed oral sex on him, and as I did so I noticed a tattoo on his left outer calf. The next thing I remember was that two other men came in from the southern entrance of the overgrown vegetation. They were both naked, and the first guy—the man I had been having oral sex with—pushed my head down into the ground. The second guy grabbed both of my ankles with his hands so that my legs were over each of his shoulders. He had his feet on the inside of my knees forcing my legs apart. The third guy lay on top of me and tried to put his penis into my anus.'

During the attack, Jones was forced to perform oral sex and lie on the ground while one of the attackers called him a 'slut' and yelled 'all poofters should be exterminated'. A cigarette lighter was applied to his scrotum and he was kicked and punched, resulting in four broken ribs, a fractured forearm and cracked vertebrae in his neck.

'I was scared for my life when the three men were raping me,' said Jones. 'I thought they were going to kill me. They said they knew who I was and where I lived and if I said anything they would be back. All three ejaculated more than once. They did not use condoms.

'When they finished, one of them masturbated over my face while another urinated on my body. The other one kicked me about the torso. They punched and kicked me before leaving.

'When they had gone, I lay there for some time. I was crying hysterically and didn't want to move. Eventually I calmed down a bit and made my way home to Carlisle Street. My mother was staying with us at the time. I told her what happened and cleaned myself up in the shower. I went to St Vincent's Hospital by taxi and was treated in emergency. I didn't tell the hospital staff anything; just that I'd been in trouble.

'I had four broken ribs, a fracture in my right forearm, two cracked vertebrae in the back of my neck, and a laceration to the back of my head which required four or five stitches and severe bruising across much of my body.

'I never went to the police because I was scared the attackers would make good on their threats to come after me.'

Whoever was behind this savage assault, Page was confident they were not responsible for the deaths of

Warren and Russell, the bashing of 'Rick', and other bashing robberies on the cliff tops. These attackers were older than any of the members of the known teenage gangs of the time—the Bondi Boys and the Alexandria Eight—then prowling the Bondi cliff tops. Secondly, the nature of the attack was radically different from any other during this period; the only thing it shared with the others, perhaps, was cold-blooded calculation.

Jones's attackers were pure sexual predators, and Page suspected they were prison-hardened ones at that, learning such homosexual violence while they were in custody.

Later that afternoon, sitting opposite Page in the interview room at Paddington Police Station, the 47-year-old gave them a thumbnail sketch of his life. He'd always known he was gay, he explained. 'I tried to be straight in my younger years. I had girlfriends and was engaged to be married three times. I finally accepted my sexual orientation when I was about 21 years old.'

He grew up in the Wollongong area and had been dressing up since he was fourteen, he said without blinking. By his late twenties he was appearing in drag in pubs and clubs, finally scoring in 1983, at the age of 29, a contract with Les Girls in Kings Cross.

Which is how he met Ross Warren in 1988. 'I had moved back to Wollongong for a while because I had a gig at Kennedy's nightclub—a straight nightclub that staged drag shows. I performed under my drag name "Sadie" and the show used to attract quite a few stars from WIN TV at the time, including Ross. There were hardly any gay venues in Wollongong back then.

'I also got to know Ross quite well because we went to the same parties and had friends in common. We weren't close friends, but we'd usually have a chat and look out for one another around the traps. Ross was strictly "in the closet" because of his career, which he put ahead of everything else.

'You know, Ross would have been horrified by all the publicity that surrounded his disappearance—being on Oxford Street that night, being last seen at a gay beat. He was always so concerned about his image, and getting to the top in the smallest amount of time. But time was what he didn't have.'

Jones paused for a moment, and then looked Page straight in the eye. 'I have only six months to live,' he declared flatly. 'I don't have an immune system anymore.'

So many people he'd been close to, friends he'd laughed with, commiserated with, were now gone. If AIDS didn't get them, the gay bashers did.

As he was being dropped back at Central Station, Jones wished Page well in the investigation and hoped he would be able to nail the monsters who killed Ross and John Russell.

The heavens opened up just after they pulled up. Walking through the cold rain along Eddy Avenue with his pullover sodden, and the bleat of peak-hour traffic in the background, the small, spindly Jones cut a lonely figure indeed.

Which is no doubt how he felt as he waited on the platform for his train back home.

9 INTO THIN AIR

'Hello, Detective Page, my name is Jacques Musy,' the caller declared in a thick French accent. Page didn't need to prompt the man with the usual preliminary questions. It was clear he had a tale he wanted to tell. Jacques had spent over seventeen years, he said, speculating on what happened to his flatmate, also a French national, who disappeared in Bondi in September 1985. And now, he said, having read about the murders and disappearances at Marks Park, and hearing from a friend about the television report of the dummy being pushed off the cliff, he might finally have an explanation.

'Gilles used to take long walks around the headland,' Jacques explained. 'One day he didn't come home. I was in France at the time, and it was left to a couple of our friends to start the search. His parents were in France, I flew back as soon as I could, but they didn't want to come. Gilles was just 27 . . .

'He'd been my partner for over seven years.'

Page promptly invited Jacques—a 55-year-old finance consultant who had been living in Australia for 23 years—into the station to make a statement.

This was a development Page hadn't anticipated, especially now that he was so advanced with the investigation into the Warren and Russell deaths. He had so many persons of interest that he had to limit how much wider he could cast his net. And he knew he might have his work cut out convincing those in the police department's executive corridors to add yet another case to Operation Taradale: officially, this investigation was about the murders of Warren, Russell and the attempted murder of 'Rick'. But he was getting a little ahead of himself . . .

A week later, Page was sitting face to face in the interview room—when it was a court house the old magistrate's office—with a slim, neatly dressed middle-aged man with receding grey hair and a polite, shy gaze.

Jacques Musy gradually felt at ease telling his story to Page, whose gentle nature seemed at odds with his solid frame and down-to-business demeanour. Although Page was circumspect in what he could actually say, Jacques never doubted his absolute commitment in hunting down the bashers and murderers of John Russell and Ross Warren—and perhaps finding out the fate of the man he once thought he would spend the rest of his life with. He held up a photo of Gilles Mattaini—a smiling shot taken only months before he disappeared—and then relayed in stark detail the events surrounding his disappearance.

◆

Gilles (pronounced 'Jeel') loved living in Bondi and enjoyed nothing more than taking long, lazy strolls along the famous, picturesque beachfront while listening to his beloved Walkman. He would pull on his favourite yellow spray jacket, jeans and sneakers, pop in his earphones and set off from their flat in Ramsgate Avenue on the Ben Buckler headland for a walk that would often take him to Tamarama and Bronte beaches to the south. He could be gone for hours, stopping at whatever spot took his fancy to watch the surf crash against the rocks, or the storm clouds roll in from the sea, while listening to the melodic, hook-filled French pop songs he adored. The legendary Françoise Hardy was one of his favourites.

'Even after all these years,' Jacques explained in his French accent, 'that music haunts me. I have to fight back the tears whenever I hear it.'

Gilles was a diminutive, shortish man, weighing no more than 60 kg, still boyish in the face at 27, with fair brown hair and bright, twinkly eyes. He was a bit of a daydreamer: a timid, softly spoken young man who devoured books, loved playing cards, enjoyed cooking and loved lounging about on the beach. 'We were like lizards in the sun,' Jacques said with a smile. The pair would grab some food and drinks, pull on their togs and beach towels and spend a whole day jumping about in the surf, sunbaking and reading, he said.

They shared a special bond, he explained—the type you find only once or twice in life if you're lucky.

'If Gilles were still alive,' he continued, 'I am sure we would still be together.'

Gilles had never been sexually promiscuous and only went to bars with Jacques and friends and never frequented beats. He drank only socially, and during the whole time they were together, Jacques never knew him to take drugs.

Growing up just north of Paris near Charles de Gaulle Airport, Gilles had endured emotional hardship. An only child, he was close to his mother and grandmother, who lived with him, but distant from his father, a factory worker who didn't show much interest in his bookish and sensitive son. At eighteen Gilles was conscripted to national service with the French Army, which he described as the most miserable time of his life.

'At his lowest point,' explained Jacques, 'he tried to take his own life with an overdose of tablets.'

Page couldn't help but cut Jacques off.

'Was he ever suicidal again after that?'

'No, he wasn't prone to depression, and never attempted suicide again,' Jacques replied. 'He found happiness in Australia—the difficult times were earlier in his life. His life became a lot happier once he left the Army and moved to Paris.'

The pair met in a Paris nightclub in the winter of 1978. Or rather, outside the club. The then 28-year-old Jacques had first spied the young man with the fine-boned features and long, light brown tousled hair standing in a queue at the entrance, huddled against the cold. Although he was hoping to run into him again on the dance floor, Gilles was nowhere to be seen.

After grabbing his coat and scarf out of the coat check, Jacques saw the young man disappear out the front door. Intrigued, he followed him to his car. Hearing footsteps, Gilles turned around and looked searchingly at Jacques before asking, 'What do you want?'

'I'm not stalking you,' Jacques smiled. 'I just wanted to say hello.'

The couple wound up chatting for over an hour, sitting in the front seat of Gilles's beaten-up old Renault to get out of the cold. 'We had an instant chemistry,' Jacques explained. 'We would spend hours talking to one another on the phone.'

Within six months, the pair were sharing a flat together with two others in Paris's Opera district. Apart from a year in Nice while he was at university studying psychology and his time doing national service, this was Gilles's biggest break yet from home. He was 20.

'We had a good life together,' reflected Jacques. 'We both worked for banks—Gilles was always good with numbers—and this paid for regular holidays to places like the Maldives and Sri Lanka.'

After five years of the grind of Paris, however, they were both ready for a sea change and started tossing around some dream destinations. 'One of Gilles's aunts was married to the then prime minister of Quebec, so in 1982 he went there for a month's holiday to test the waters, so to speak,' explained Jacques. 'His aunt offered to help us get jobs, find a place and sort out immigration.'

But Gilles—never a fan of cold weather—went off the idea of moving to Canada after learning the mercury can drop down to 20 below in the depths of winter. Jacques too, having grown up on Africa's Ivory Coast—his parents shifted to French-speaking Senegal in the early 1950s to work for a company—also hankered after a sun-drenched locale.

That's when the idea of coming to Australia popped up. One of their flatmates, Antony Wyszinski, had a friend, Vincent Ottaviani, who had come to Sydney, fallen in love with the climate and culture and decided to stay. Ottaviani had waxed lyrical about how tolerant Australia was, how gay people weren't afraid to be open at work, how much less formal everything seemed. 'You can even call your boss by his first name,' he enthused.

The language provided no problems, as Jacques and Gilles could both speak English fluently. And they could live by the ocean, a long-cherished dream for both of them. All roads thus seemed to lead to Sydney. They settled on a plan: Jacques would come out first, get a job and set up an apartment, and if all went well Gilles would follow some months later.

When Jacques flew into Sydney in September 1983, his first priorities were to get accommodation and a job. The ever-obliging Ottaviani offered him a room in the run-down but airy three-storey terrace house he was renting on South Dowling Street. All Jacques had to do in exchange was some light domestic duties. Within a month or so, Ottaviani, then head of banqueting at the Menzies Hotel near Wynyard Station, got Jacques a job as a barman at the hotel, and after several more months he was able to set up a casual position for Gilles as well.

So on a sunny Saturday morning, March 17, 1984, Gilles disembarked at Sydney Airport. As he came through Customs, pushing his luggage trolley in front of him and looking searchingly across the sea of faces in the arrivals area, Jacques happily snapped away with his camera for a few seconds before waving wildy in his direction. Those photographs, of a jet-lagged but full-of-expectation Gilles, surveying the crowd in a new country, continue to haunt Jacques to this day, he said.

Within a matter of weeks the pair were spending every spare moment flat-hunting in the beachside suburbs of Bondi and Tamarama. They finally settled on a one-bedroom flat with a sunroom in a 1940s block at 11/110 Ramsgate Avenue in Bondi, commanding a panoramic view of the beach from the sash windows of the living room.

The couple relished the freedoms and outdoors lifestyle of Australia, joining the crowds on Bondi Beach in summer, bopping on the dance floor during the annual Mardi Gras party, laughing along to the drag shows at the Albury Hotel on Oxford Street and dining out with friends and colleagues in Darlinghurst and Paddington. Late in 1984 they had a short holiday together in Bali.

Over takeaway fish and chips one night Gilles told Jacques he had never been happier. By August 1985 he was becoming a little anxious, however, about the approaching expiry of his visa. But he wasn't growing an ulcer over it because management at the Menzies Hotel suggested they might sponsor him. Like Jacques, he had decided to take up residency.

On Friday August 16, Jacques climbed on a plane to Paris for a five-week visit to family and old friends, including Antony Wyszynski, who had been made redundant in his job and was planning to move to Australia in October. The three planned to share the Bondi flat together until Wyszynski became established and found a place for himself.

Jacques spoke to Gilles once or twice a week while he was away. Gilles was so excited about Wyszynski's forthcoming stay that he had gone on a mini shopping spree, buying new bedding, rugs, a couple of table lamps and pot plants. In a phone conversation with Jacques only three days before he disappeared, he described his purchases and enthused about how smart the place was looking.

The last contact Gilles had with any of his friends was on the morning of Sunday September 15. He had spoken to Wyszynski on the phone and seemed to be in excellent spirits. 'Antony, I can't wait to see you,' he said as the call wound up.

At 3 p.m. the following day, Gilles didn't turn up for his eight-hour shift at the Menzies.

Ottaviani was immediately concerned. Gilles was always so punctual and would have called had he been ill. Ottaviani called the flat twice, maybe three times. No answer. He called again later in the evening. The next morning, he went over to the unit and knocked on the door. He phoned mutual friends, and then hospitals and the police station. Nothing. Later that afternoon, he called Jacques in Paris.

Jacques's descent into hell had begun. He was locked in to flying back on September 23 and couldn't change his ticket. He hardly slept for days, and dipped in and out of an exhausted sleep on the flight back to Sydney.

Jet-lagged, and with his heart racing from apprehension, Jacques walked through Customs on the sunny Tuesday afternoon of September 24, and got a taxi to Bondi. His legs almost buckled under him as he put the key in his front door and faced the silence—the emptiness—of the flat.

He did a quick check. No sign of forced entry. Everything in its usual place, barring the two new rugs and lamps Gilles had bought. All valuables intact. On the coffee table Gilles's wallet and the watch he had recently bought duty free. Nothing unusual about that. Gilles made it a habit to leave his wallet and valuables behind when he went on one of his seaside walks.

His passport was in its usual drawer.

No sign of a note.

The first thing Jacques noticed when he picked through Gilles's wardrobe, looking for any hints at where he might be, was that his Walkman and spray jacket were missing. He later found that a sloppy joe, sweat pants and a pair of runners were also gone.

Hanging on the kitchen wall was the Ken Done calendar they had bought together at Christmas. Gilles had circled the dates of his upcoming shifts at the Menzies, with the starting times scribbled in beside.

There were no entries after Monday September 16.

That afternoon, desperate for any crumb of information he could get, Jacques knocked on his neighbour's door. The tall, thirtysomething man said the last time he had seen Gilles was on the afternoon of Sunday September 15. Gilles seemed normal, if a little stand-offish.

For those first convulsive, traumatic weeks following his return to Australia, Jacques ran on autopilot, trying to distract himself with work as best he could, taking long, lonely walks along the beach, up along the headland, half-expecting to see his lover turn some corner. He lay awake at night, casting for reasons why Gilles might have committed suicide—and if he did, how he could manage to hide his body so successfully.

He asked himself if Gilles was harbouring some secret pain that wouldn't go away; that underneath the smiles there had been something deep and troubling going on.

Maybe, contrary to what he said, he had never been happy.

There were moments when Jacques cursed himself. If he hadn't gone to France, Gilles might well still be alive, he reasoned. There were other times when he thought Gilles might have run away with a new lover, which raised the hope that he would some day come back. But Jacques knew in his bones that the Gilles he had been living with for seven years wouldn't do something like that. At work, when he could contain his misery no more, he would take refuge in the loo or a storage room and burst into tears.

Dosed up on Valium to fight off his emotional slide, it was largely left to Ottaviani and Wyszynski (who arrived in Australia on October 2, earlier than planned) to continue the search, which virtually turned them into part-time detectives. They contacted everyone and every institution they could think of, from local hospitals to the French Consulate, learning the hard way that when it comes to missing people, it's like looking for a needle in a haystack. Ottaviani lodged a missing persons report with the Bondi police.

After weeks of fruitless searching, the two friends were soothing but honest with Jacques: it seemed highly unlikely that Gilles would turn up. For them, the question boiled down to whether he had met with foul play or committed suicide, and they had no leads on either.

Time marched on. Wyszynski decided to remain in Australia and gained citizenship in 1986. He stayed with Jacques in the Ramsgate Avenue apartment for the next seven years before Jacques moved to Tamarama.

It was Wyszynski, Jacques explained, who had seen the re-enactment on the telly and suggested they should contact the police. Only a few months after Gilles's disappearance, Wyszynski had seen a few young toughs chase a gay guy across Marks Park, but it didn't occur to him that the same fate could have befallen his friend.

The possibility that Giles was a murder victim rather than a suicide offered Jacques little solace, he told Page. But at least it was a plausible explanation for his confounding disappearance. And some measure of finality. 'It was a dream for us to make a new life in Australia and it was taken away,' Jacques said poignantly.

Page knew he needed all the luck he could get with this case. A fifteen-year-old disappearance, nearly four years before the major wave of fatal attacks began. A disappearance that offered no explanation, let alone any obvious clues. No police investigation at all; at least with the Warren and Russell murders, he had something to work with. No items that could identify Mattaini from DNA. Not even a record of a missing persons report, although Ottaviani had been adamant to Jacques that he had reported Gilles's disappearance to the Bondi police. No surprise there—Ross Warren's missing persons report had also gone missing. It had become a tediously familiar story.

Ottaviani could no longer help with enquiries, Jacques said, as he had passed away from AIDS only the year before. And Wyszynski, too, was now ill, but keen to help the investigation in any way he could. When he was interviewed some days later Wyszynski added a sad postscript to the tragedy: he told of his trip to France in

1986, when he visited Gilles's parents to give them some of their son's possessions. His father had long disowned Gilles because of his homosexuality and his mother preferred to think he had committed suicide rather than met with foul play. Their only child was dead, but life had already seemed to have moved on.

It was impossible to know from the outset whether this was a suicide or another murder, but Page chose to keep an open mind. There was certainly more than a whiff of foul play. In Page's experience, people who suicide usually make some attempt to get their life in order in the days prior: leave a note, close bank accounts, allow work commitments to fall away. Gilles had spent money on furnishing their apartment, he had been in a jovial mood on the phone the day he disappeared, he was looking forward to a visit from a close friend—these actions didn't fit the pattern of a man about to kill himself.

So for the moment, at least, Page could only continue under one assumption: that the treacherous cliffs at Bondi had claimed another victim.

While he thought it highly unlikely that Mattaini's death was part of the drumbeat of attacks that occurred between 1988 and 1990, it was just possible that the killers of Warren and Russell might know or have some connection with an earlier bunch of bashers. When Page's assistant checked the records, he found that there had indeed been a spasm of anti-gay attacks across the inner city in mid 1985.

The danger zone at the time, however, seemed to be the laneways behind Oxford Street rather than the cliff tops. In the early hours of a Saturday morning on

June 15, 1985, a male dancer was killed in a lonely back street of Darlinghurst, after being set upon by seven young men who called him a 'poofter' and 'faggot'. One attacker held the dancer's legs so that the others could kick his head and upper body. He was left unconscious, bleeding from the nose and mouth, and breathing oddly. An unidentified transsexual who witnessed the attack tried to comfort him. He was taken to nearby St Vincent's Hospital but never regained consciousness, dying ten days later from severe head injuries.

Page was critically short of information on Gilles's death, and so appealed to the public—once again—with any details they could provide. Press releases were drawn up and Page spoke to two newspaper journalists.

A few days later the following story appeared in Sydney's *The Daily Telegraph*:

> POLICE believe the disappearance of a French man in Sydney more than a decade ago may be related to a spate of gay bashings and murders in the 1980s. Gilles Mattaini, a 27-year-old gay Bondi resident, was last seen in September, 1985. Police yesterday revealed his unexplained disappearance could be related to other assaults on gay men at Tamarama in the city's eastern suburbs. 'An investigation has been launched to establish what may have happened,' Sergeant Page said. 'We're not saying it's definitely linked [to gay-hate gangs] at this stage but we're keeping an open mind about it.' A reward of up to $1000 has been posted for information leading to an arrest.

So who killed Gilles Mattaini?

Page had no idea, but the investigation was at least making some strides regarding the Warren and Russell deaths. He now had a clear sense of the principal gangs in the late 1980s targeting gay men. They were the Alexandria Eight (who killed Richard Johnson, and possibly William Allen); the Tamarama Three (who murdered Kritchikorn Rattanajurathaporn); and the Bondi Boys (who allegedly attempted to kill Rick, among a host of other crimes at the cliff tops). Under the Bondi Boys, Page had a list of ten names, corroborated by witness statements and police reports of the time. All these gangs were prolific in gay bashings, the murders representing the mere peak of their hard-knuckled attacks.

Page was now finding his way through the frustrating fog that enveloped the connections between the gangs. This much he already knew: Sean Cushman, leader of the Bondi Boys, knew David McAuliffe, one of Rattanajurathaporn's killers. Matthew Davis, another of Rattanajurathaporn's killers, had also indicated that his mate David McAuliffe hung out with 'Cushy' (Cushman), even though Davis hadn't met him. It was also clear that Ronald Morgan—one of Richard Johnson's killers—also knew the McAuliffes, as they'd grown up together in the Waterloo area.

The records revealed other connections. One of the women who provided an alibi for the men involved in the bashing of Robert at Centennial Park just before Christmas in 1988 was living with Mark Church at the time he (along with two others) was convicted of murdering Richard Johnson in Alexandria Park.

And through his team of detectives, Page was learning more and more about the notorious Bondi Boys. Former member 'AJ' made a statement concerning a recent conversation he had with his old Bondi Boys mate Richard Porter, and an unidentified man—a statement that was tabled at the later inquest. They were seated at the breakfast table in Norman Andrews House, a drop-in centre in Roscoe Street, Bondi, and discussing another former Bondi Boys member, Graham Holmes.

As soon as 'AJ' mentioned Holmes, Porter got angry and declared: 'He's had to leave. The cops have spoken to him. He dobbed us in. The cops put the hard word on him. They are going to talk to all of us now. Remember those poofs that got pushed off the cliff about ten years ago? We were the Bondi Killers. The PTK. There are not many of us around anymore. We were just mucking around, we grabbed one of them and pushed him, we pushed him back and he just fell off the cliff . . . Some newsreader from Wollongong.'

Richard Porter then added, 'We got quite a few of them, but one of them got away and talked to police.'

'AJ' said he knew Porter was talking about the murders at Marks Park, as the reopening of the investigation had been all over the papers in the previous weeks. 'I was trying to pretend I didn't hear anything, but I was shitting myself,' said 'AJ'. 'The other guy was in shock too and we didn't know what to do. So when the time was right we just got up and said goodbye.'

A constable who had performed general duties at Bondi patrol in 1988 also recalled having a conversation with one of the members of the Bondi Boys, Robert Jewell, at a unit in Moore Street, Bondi. He recalled

Jewell saying that 'the Bondi Boys threw a poofter off the cliff at South Bondi'. The constable had the impression that Jewell had seen the event. He submitted an information report on this at the time.

But when Jewell was tracked down and interviewed, he flatly denied being a member of the Bondi Boys, even if he knew a couple of its members, including Cushman. Jewell claimed that he did not remember ever saying to a police officer, 'the Bondi Boys threw a poofter off the cliff at Bondi', and if he did it was empty boasting.

Tough talk is cheap when you're young and trying to impress your mates. Page knew that separating the truth from the braggadocio would be incredibly hard. And yet . . . the stories of the Bondi Boys 'pushing a poofter over a cliff' had now come from four different sources. Add the fact that its members had a long, ignoble record of bashing gay men at Bondi and this gave strong grounds for suspicion.

Page had the sense that he still needed more 'insider' information.

10 A CITY'S SHAME

Did you kill John Russell? Were you there when Ross Warren was attacked? Do you know who murdered these men? Like any good detective, Page knew the value of leaving the most simple and direct questions to last when interviewing a suspect or person of interest—the real art is in the questions that precede it. So on a sweaty summer afternoon in early December 2001, he was busily nutting out individual questions for each of the fifteen persons of interest who were about to be interviewed.

There is no more practised liar, of course, than the one who has been on the wrong side of the law a few times. The interviews that Page had organised, months in the planning, were to be timed so that suspects were caught off guard, and had as little opportunity as possible to talk to one another, share alibis and swap stories. Nearly seventeen months into the investigation, Page still didn't know as much as he would have liked about the web of connections between the three gangs who launched deadly attacks on gay men in the late 1980s. He was determined to crack open a few cans to see what crawled out.

Again, Page reminded himself of the established facts of the case—contained in arrest reports, witness statements and lawfully obtained recordings. The Bondi Boys were involved in a host of ferocious bashings around the beachfront area and Marks Park in 1988, 1989 and 1990. Sean Cushman, alleged leader of the Bondi Boys, was a mate of David McAuliffe, one of Rattanajurathaporn's killers and a member of the Tamarama Three. Two other gay men identified Cushman as being one of the principal perpetrators in their bashings in late 1989 and early 1990, including 'Rick', who was allegedly threatened with, 'I'm going to throw you over the side.'

There were also links between one or two members of the Alexandria Eight and the Tamarama Three. It was clear that Ronald Morgan—a member of the Alexandria Eight—knew the McAuliffe brothers, from living close to one another in Waterloo.

What remained murky was the extent to which any members of the Bondi Boys, Alexandria Eight or Tamarama Three were directly involved in, or had knowledge of, the deaths of Warren and Russell.

Now that Page had a comprehensive list of Bondi Boys members, he found out that two of them were later involved in a murder in Alexandria in January 1992. A merchant seaman and father of two, Noel Doull, was bashed and robbed outside the Camellia Grove Hotel in Henderson Road, Alexandria, only ten minutes walk from Alexandria Park, where William Allen and Richard Johnson were killed. Doull was in a coma for a week at

Royal Prince Alfred Hospital before his life support system was turned off with his twenty-year-old son Bart by his side, who made an impassioned appeal to the public to help find his father's killers.

'I just hope they regret what they have done and get caught,' he said.

It was only a matter of days before the two boys—part of a group of six—were appearing at Glebe Coroner's Court charged with murder. One, who lived in Alexandria, was only fifteen; the other, aged seventeen, lived in Bondi.

Sean Cushman had no involvement in the Doull attack. But in 1996 he was charged with being an accessory after the fact in the murder of British tourist Brian Hagland, so Page set out to obtain a full set of the court transcripts.

His team had now scouted widely for former members of the Bondi Boys, the Alexandria Eight and the Tamarama Three. Some were in jail, but most had melted back into society, not just in the suburbs of Sydney, but also regional NSW. Page had already waded through the swamp of legal procedures required to get certain persons of interest interviewed and recorded.

The wave of interviews began in earnest in mid December 2001. Page fully expected the usual limp 'I don't know anything' responses. What he was looking out for were those who didn't want to talk, and those whose stories were suspiciously incomplete—in short, anyone who looked like they were hiding something. The prize, of course, would be some clear-cut, incriminating statements.

Then it would be up to the coroner to decide whether any of the interview material should be brought to trial.

◆

On Monday December 17, two of Page's colleagues interviewed Ronald Morgan at a police station on the NSW Central Coast. They had been directed to ask not just about the Bondi murders but the slaying of retired school teacher William Allen in Alexandria Park in December 1988, a year before Morgan and his mates killed Johnson. Although the Allen murder was not officially part of Operation Taradale, Page thought the bugged conversation between Morgan and Dean Howard at Minda Detention Centre in April 1991, in which they seemed to imply that other members of the gang killed Allen, could not be overlooked. Interestingly, another tape from the same period, in which French discussed the Allen killing, alleged Morgan was involved.

Page provided the interviewing Central Coast detectives with the transcripts and tapes, highlighting the two relevant sections, in which the pair described this earlier bashing, one that sounded so suspiciously similar to the Allen murder. Location, the nature of the school teacher's death, all matched. Although Morgan and Howard recall the murder happening in 1989, it was an easy mistake to make, as Allen was killed at the very end of 1988, three days after Christmas.

> Howard: 'It fuckin' scares me mate, 'cause you know, the next one, if we get done for another one that ends up with life.'
> Morgan: 'Yeah, I know.'
> 'Fuck, all those unsolved murders up there. Yeah, this other one…'
> 'That was in 1989.'
> 'What, our one?'

'Ours was 1990.'
'Yeah, he crawled home and died in a coma, that other bloke that was in the fuckin' paper.'
Howard: 'I know Brad and Churchy was involved. Who else is involved? 'Cause I want to talk to 'em mate.'
'How did he die?'
'...his home, he just bled to death.'
'Yeah.'
'You'd never believe 'em because that was supposed to be the most horrendous bashing in history.'
'Fuck.'
'And then, now ours is supposed to be the most horrific.'
'They reckon somewhere along the line they stabbed him with a screwdriver.'
'Fuck, they're fuckin' idiots.'
'And now they put all the shit on us, we're in enough shit.'

The interview began with questions about Warren and Russell. Morgan insisted he had no idea who killed either, or who attempted to kill 'Rick'. He insisted he never went to Bondi after nightfall, and didn't throw anyone off a cliff. Yes, he knew Sean and David McAuliffe, the murderers of Kritchikorn Rattanajurathaporn. They used to meet up to play footy or cricket in the park between their units. Their paths also crossed again while they were in jail. But he said he had no knowledge of the Bondi Boys or their members.

At that point the detective pressed the button on the 1991 tape in which William Allen's murder was apparently being discussed.

The detective turned to Morgan and asked, 'Do you know what "Allen" bloke they're referring to?'

'No, definitely not,' he replied.

The detective inserted another tape into the machine,

this one of Adam French boasting about the bashings in 1991:

> 'And then Morgan hit him across the head with a sledgehammer...'

Detective: 'What have you got to say about that?'

'I don't know: I've never hit anyone with a sledgehammer!'

The detective rewound the tape a little, to the beginning of French's description of the attack on the man called Allen.

> 'Yeah, they go up to him and go, "What do you go for?"... Morgan said, "Don't talk because you're dead" and then they hit him across the mouth with a sledgehammer...'

'Did you at any time approach a person and say, "Don't talk because you're dead?"'

'No, definitely not.'

Detective: 'Is there any reason why [French] would say that?'

'I'm sorry, that's just got me. I find that just a bit strange and he seems to know the bloke's name. I certainly didn't, I certainly don't . . . that one there that got killed, that Allen bloke . . . off the sheet, is what Howard said. He seems to know a bit.'

Morgan, who had spent 10 years in jail, told the Central Coast detectives that he no longer mixed with any of the group. His sister and brother had long since packed up the family house in Alexandria, which was adjacent to the park, to escape the 'bad influence' of the neighbourhood, and had shifted out of the city.

While Morgan was being interviewed on the NSW Central Coast, Alex Mihailovic, convicted of Johnson's manslaughter, was interviewed at Redfern Police Station. He was shown pictures of Warren and Russell, but Mihailovic insisted he did not recognise them and had never been to Marks Park.

Meanwhile at Waverley Police Station, another former Bondi Boys member, Justin King, was being interviewed. He was nicknamed 'Sharkhead', he explained, because he was the only member of the group who surfed. He had only been to Marks Park once, he said, about four years earlier, to play a game of cricket. 'I didn't even know it [the park] was there,' he said.

'Did you know it was a gay beat?' asked Page.

'No,' he replied.

Page pushed a number of newspaper clippings about the Warren and Russell deaths in front of him.

'I don't remember reading or hearing about this, sir,' said King politely. 'It's only recently that it was in the paper. It's the only time I have heard about it.'

King had heard of the Park Side Killers moniker, but thought it related to a 'mob in Maroubra'. He had never been a member of the PSK, he claimed.

The next day, another of Richard Johnson's murderers, Dean Howard, was asked to come into Maroubra Police Station. However, he refused to participate in a recorded interview or supply a statement. 'I don't know anything about them,' he said of the Warren and Russell deaths. He then refused to answer any further questions.

Another man mentioned on Adam French's tapes, Sam Maarraoui, was interviewed by Page at Paddington Police Station. He staunchly denied any involvement in the Russell and Warren deaths.

Page then said: 'I also want to interview you in relation to a lawfully obtained listening-device product which suggests you were involved in the serious assault of a gay male where he was made to extinguish a cigarette on his penis.'

'I have nothing to say,' replied Sam Maarraoui, who then declined to make a formal statement or even to sign a notebook on the conversations they had.

◆

Page had organised for former first-grade rugby league player Darrell Trindall to be interviewed at Mascot Police Station a few days earlier, on Thursday 13 December 2001. While Trindall was not a suspect in the murders of Russell and Warren, he did associate with several known gay-bashers of the time, and had been implicated by Adam French in an assault at Centennial Park.

There was also the charge against him in 1989, also at Centennial Park, for obstructing police as they arrested two of his mates for a gay bashing. Page wanted to pin down exactly how much Trindall knew about the shenanigans of the Alexandria Eight—after all, he went to school with them—and other gay-bashers of the time.

Trindall sighed when the detective at Maroubra station asked him to recall the events of that period. He was at Cleveland Street Boys High for two years, he said, played football in Alexandria Park, and knew Adam

French, Ron Morgan and Brad Young from school and footy, but didn't know they were members of a gang and hadn't seen any of them in more than twelve years.

Trindall said he had never been to Marks Park, hadn't heard of the PSK, although he seemed to recall another acronym, PIC, or Partners in Crime, which he thought referred to a gang active around his own neighbourhood in Waterloo.

Page then provided a transcript of the 1991 tape recording of Adam French at Keelong Detention Centre in which he described a gay bashing at Centennial Park, where 'Trindall pissed in a gay man's wig'.

'Did you ever bash anyone in any gang or group?' the detective asked.

'We probably have had some fights when we were young,' Trindall replied. 'And probably being young hoods, hanging together. But I never frequented the gay places.'

Trindall knew at the time that French and seven others were arrested for the murder of Richard Johnson in Alexandria Park, but claimed he 'didn't know they actually went out bashing gays and set out on 'em.'

But these guys were mates of yours, Page pointed out, surely you knew what they were up to?

'After it [Johnson's murder] happened, I don't know who the first one was, but one of the guys got arrested and it just spread around our area that there was a lot of them that was goin' to get done for it.'

◆

Several weeks afterwards, on a rainy humid morning in

early 2002, Page drove down to Port Kembla on the NSW South Coast to interview Adam French.

After being shown photographs of Ross Warren and John Russell, French claimed he had not seen either of them before, and had no knowledge of their deaths. He knew nothing about the attempted murder of 'Rick', he claimed.

He was familiar with the coastal pathway between Tamarama and Bondi, he explained, from his days as a lifeguard on Bronte Beach, and from surfing at Bondi.

'When were you a lifeguard at Bronte?' Page asked.

'In 1987 and 1988,' he replied, 'when I was about 15 and 16.'

French claimed he had never been at the cliff tops after nightfall—in summer, no later than 8.30 p.m.— because at the time he lived with his grandmother in Waterloo.

At that moment Page pushed the button on the tape recorder, in which French's voice could be heard boasting to Dean Howard how he and several mates bashed a gay man with a skateboard and pushed him off a small cliff, before stealing his car keys.

'That,' said Page, 'was what you said back in 1991 at Keelong Detention Centre.'

French swiftly dismissed it as 'skylarkin', boasting . . . but I'd say some of it happened, yeah.'

French wasn't happy about the fact he had been recorded.

'The conversation was lawfully recorded as a result of a warrant issued by the Supreme Court judge,' Page explained. Page then put it to French that this crime had parallels to the deaths of Russell and Warren, but French insisted he didn't see or attack either of those two men.

'I'm sure we never pushed anyone off a cliff that didn't get back up—that cliff wasn't that high,' said French. 'Like I said on the tape... the guy got up screamin'.'

French paused for a moment. 'No-one went off any high cliff or entered any water.'

Their line of attack, French explained, was to beat a victim, 'grab his keys, run back up to the car, search his car', looking mainly for money. In the assault described on the tape, he 'didn't really get anything so I tossed his keys into the water near the swimming pool'.

Back then, French continued, he had made a habit of collecting newspaper clippings of 'incidents' he was involved in, but he'd since lost them. Which may go some way to explaining why, during the course of the interview, he mixed up the name of the man he and his mates killed in Alexandria Park. He called Richard Johnson 'Michael', and dismissed the murder as 'an assault that went pretty wrong and ended up in death'.

French vehemently denied having any association with the Bondi Boys, being a member of a graffiti gang, or knowing what the letters 'PTK' stood for. Despite strong hints in the 1991 recording that he knew who was behind the Russell killing, he now claimed he really knew nothing.

◆

Yet another man mentioned on the French tapes, Justin Pope, was interviewed at Nambucca Heads Police Station on the NSW North Coast. Quizzed about the deaths of John Russell and Ross Warren, he claimed not to have heard of either of these men, nor to have been involved in attacks in the Marks Park area. While he admitted to knowing Adam French and Justin King, he said he had never heard of the Park Side Killers or People That Kill.

However, a former Bondi Boys member, Ned Hadjukovic, interviewed at Hurstville Police Station, was a little more forthcoming. Sean Cushman, Timothy Alger, Joseph Phillips and Daniel Frier all went under the moniker of PSK or PTK, 'Park Side Killers or Park Crime Killers, something like that' and were a younger part of the group, he said. There were two 'crews', he added, and they used to fight among themselves.

Hadjukovic, who used to surf at South Bondi, knew Marks Park was a gay beat, and saw people being beaten up in the area, but was never involved. He has gay friends now, he emphasised.

The interview with Timothy Alger went far less smoothly. When Page arrived at Miranda Police Station for the interview, Alger was ensconced in the charge room, faced with a separate offence. He refused to be interviewed about gay bashings at Bondi or the Warren and Russell deaths, bellowing 'I haven't done anything wrong. I don't know anything about these poofter bashings. I will get a good lawyer and fight it in court.'

Meanwhile, Senior Constable Robert Wood, who was a member of the Bondi patrol in the late 1980s, confirmed in a police statement to Page that Cushman, Alger and Phillips regularly hung out together and were charged with a variety of offences at the time, including some involving violence.

Matthew Davis was interviewed at Campbelltown Police Station. He said he became mates with the McAuliffe brothers while living in the Sydney suburb of Clovelly in 1987 and 1988. Although he admitted being a graffiti artist at that time, he claimed he had never used and did not know what the tag PSK stood for.

'Is it the case,' asked the detective, 'that Sean and David McAuliffe told you back then they had committed other offences at Bondi?'

'Yeah. There may have been some teenage bravado. They didn't say Marks Park, just Bondi. "We did a roll the other week", and you know what I mean, and that was it.'

'The Thai national, how did he meet his death?' enquired the detective.

'He was backing away and was, like he's gone, there's the cliff face there like that and as he's backing away he's fallen off the edge of the cliff and then apparently he's hit a ledge, and then he's gone off that and ended up in the water.'

The detective jumped straight to the point.

'Did you kill Ross Warren?'

'No, I did not.'

'Did you kill John Russell?'

'No, I did not.'

'Were you present when either Ross Warren or John Russell were killed?'

'No.'

'Do you know who killed Ross Warren or John Russell?'

'No, I do not.'

But some weeks after the interview, Matthew Davis came knocking on the door of the police again—this time with much more compelling details about the night Kritchikorn Rattanajurathaporn was murdered.

After the trio left the cliff tops and returned to the flat in Redfern, Davis said he was a 'mess'.

'I saw Rattanajurathaporn fall from the cliff . . . and I was hoping he was all right. I was shitting myself about being caught and going to jail. I noticed that Sean and David McAuliffe were really relaxed and did not show any signs of being upset whatsoever.'

Davis further alleged that David McAuliffe had said words to the effect of: 'Don't worry, brother. This isn't the first time we have done this. You're one of us now. Just ask Sean and Cushy.'

Davis said he didn't know Cushy. 'I had heard David speak of Cushy before, he was a friend of theirs, and he was described as being "a tall lanky prick, a hard nut".'

David and Sean McAuliffe, still in jail for Rattanajurathaporn's murder, refused to cooperate with the investigation, which led Page to organise lawful listening devices.

◆

David McAuliffe's mate Sean Cushman had come under the notice of the police 32 times between March 28, 1987 and May 1, 1992. One department report noted that he had shown nothing but contempt for the police and the courts, and their ability to put him behind bars.

Maybe for good reason. In 1996, Cushman was arrested over the assault and death of 28-year-old British tourist Brian Hagland at Bondi Beach. In a controversial decision that had Hagland's girlfriend and his father blasting what they saw as a 'kangaroo court', Cushman later got off with a good behaviour bond and his mate Aaron Martin with a minimum sentence of two years and three months. After both were charged with murder, Martin was found guilty only of the lesser charge of causing grievous bodily harm, and Cushman of assisting after the fact.

Page spent several hours poring over the case notes. Cushman and Martin had been sauntering past Hagland, who was walking hand in hand with his girlfriend on Campbell Parade, when Martin made a crude comment about the young woman's breasts.

'What did you say?' Hagland asked, before Martin turned back and savagely struck him. Once he had Hagland on the ground, Martin pummelled into him with kicks and punches, before grabbing his neck and—according to the prosecution—throwing him into the side of an oncoming bus.

Only a few minutes earlier, Hagland, a London postman and up-and-coming rock musician, had been carrying a bouquet of flowers for his girlfriend. Now she was left cradling her lover's head in her arms as he lay dying on the roadside, the flowers scattered nearby. The couple had been together for more than seven years, had spent the previous eight months travelling around Australia, and were due to fly out to New Zealand two days later. They planned to get married once they returned to London.

Martin's solicitor—chic, high-profile lawyer Leigh Johnson—convinced the court that this was a simple, tragic case of 'testosterone poisoning': an altercation that spun out of control between two hot-headed young men who 'have a few drinks, have a scuffle'. Martin's barrister, Peter Bodor, claimed self-defence, successfully convincing the jury that 'at no time did he intend to kill or seriously injure Mr Hagland'.

In the eyes of the jury, the explanation that Hagland's death was due to a mix of 'testosterone poisoning' and the demon of binge drinking seemed entirely plausible. They didn't know that Cushman was suspected of being involved in other assaults; they didn't know Martin had served a fifteen-month jail term for a savage attack only three years earlier. To them, this was a one-off tragic fight between two men caught up in a classic alpha-male showdown, where one of them—Martin—suddenly snapped.

But it was a fight waiting to happen. The court was told how the heavily intoxicated Martin put his fist through the glass pane of a toilet door at the North Bondi RSL Club, threatened to throw a stool at the bar, and upon leaving the club with Cushman, smashed the glass door of a nearby restaurant. As the pair made their way down the street, Martin, whose hair-trigger temper had got him into many scrapes before, harassed a couple of passers-by and smeared the blood from his hands—torn up by the glass of the toilet door—across several shop windows.

And then the pair saw the floppy-haired, six-foot-two Brian Hagland—whom friends described as a gentle giant—hand in hand with his pretty girlfriend, only metres up the road. The couple had been for farewell drinks with colleagues from the Australian Trade Commission, where Hagland's girlfriend, Connie Casey, had worked.

Page read Casey's description of what happened next, and what the prosecution described as Cushman's cold and cowardly indifference during it:

> One of the men just bounded straight up to Brian and punched the top of his chest. Brian grabbed at the man's hand to push him away and said, 'Look, I don't want any trouble'.
>
> But the man just pushed down on Brian with all his weight so that Brian's head was in the gutter.
>
> His friend [Cushman] had walked behind me and gone to stand on the end of the road by Bondi Beach. I just started screaming and looking at his friend, asking for help. He just looked away.
>
> I became hysterical, screaming and screaming, hoping that somebody in the nearby flats would hear and help. I went over to Brian, screaming his name. I noticed he was unconscious because I could only see the whites of his eyes.
>
> The only parts of his body that were moving were his feet. They were moving so feebly but he was trying to push off this man who was lying on top of him. Then I saw the man had both hands around Brian's throat . . .

The horrified Casey, her entreaties ignored by Cushman, saw no other alternative but to leave the scene and race into the nearest cafe for help. While she was away, the prosecution argued, Martin pushed Hagland into the path of a passing bus. They further alleged that Martin repeatedly kicked Hagland's head as he lay dying. Whether Martin committed such heinous acts or not, autopsy results revealed that Hagland's injuries from the fight were so severe that it's unlikely he would have survived them.

After returning to the scene with assistance, Casey bent down and touched her partner's hand. 'But he was just making a moan, like a low "ooooh", and a spray of blood was coming from his nose and mouth onto the road.'

Cushman's only response during the whole ordeal was to hail a taxi to remove him and Martin from the scene. Four days later, after the story hit the papers and Casey made an emotional plea on the evening news for the killer and his accomplice to be caught, the pair turned themselves in to the police.

In court Cushman claimed that because of an operation on his hand two months earlier, he was powerless to break up the fight. 'I couldn't risk getting it injured,' he said. Why a sore hand should stop him from calling off his friend or seeking help he failed to explain to the court.

What Page didn't know from reading the case notes was that the verdict and sentencing in July 1999 drew outraged newspaper headlines, not only in Sydney, but in newspapers across Britain. 'Bondi attacker cleared of murder' exclaimed *The Times*. 'Mum's agony as Aussie thug gets off murder rap' declared *The Sun*.

As the full impact of the verdict and sentencing sank in, Hagland's girlfriend was inconsolable. 'He [Aaron Martin] has got away with murder,' Casey told reporters, breaking down in tears. 'He's laughing up his sleeve at us. Meanwhile, the man I loved—still love—is gone. He was my soul mate and I shall never get over losing him.'

Hagland's father, Brian Hagland Senior, described the court case as an 'absolute shambles'.

Because of the time he had already served on remand in prison, Martin was eligible for parole just fourteen months later. The police, community and politicians appealed the verdict, but to no avail.

Page was interested by another police record dated November 1999. Cushman turned up at a house in Bondi and spoke to the mother of Daniel McDonald. Cushman was hostile and said he was representing Ned Hadjukovic (who was serving a custodial sentence) and that her son owed more than $23 000 as payment for drugs. She told him she didn't know where her son was, and that he had paid $3000 in August 1998. Cushman then boasted that he had killed a man in Bondi and had got away with it and would do so again because the 'coppers are too fuckin' stupid'. He threatened future harm to her son before turning around and swaggering off.

◆

When Cushman was called into the station, he was polite and reserved, but seemed nervous, Page noted.

'I wish to interview you in relation to the suspicious deaths of Ross Warren and John Russell, together with the attempted murder of "Rick" [his real name inserted], all of which occurred at Tamarama in 1989,' Page calmly informed Cushman.

'I want to talk, but I don't want to be interviewed at the moment until I can speak with my solicitor,' Cushman replied.

Cushman's lawyer later rang Page and said her client would not participate in an interview regarding the deaths at Bondi.

Cushman's refusal to cooperate, combined with evidence from other interviews with suspects, led to a surveillance and phone-tapping operation approved by the Supreme Court. Conversations between Cushman and his mother and a few of his mates were lawfully recorded. In one conversation Cushman joked about the possibility that the cops were listening in, suggesting he might be choosing his words carefully. In any case the recordings added little if nothing to the investigation.

In one phone conversation, Cushman's mother tells him that she had a visit from two detectives who wanted to speak about something that happened 'way back in 1989'.

'There was a couple of gay guys killed or pushed off the cliff—cliffs at Tamarama, and the dead man had a clump of blond hair and you're a suspect . . .'

Cushman laughs. 'I tell you I've got nothing to do with this, mate, all right.' His mother then asks Cushman to swear on his son's life, and he replies, 'yes'.

His mother replies, 'Oh, what a relief.'

In a later conversation, following another visit from the detectives, Cushman's mother asks him, 'Are you sure you never went up there [Marks Park] with a group of people . . . you know, giving fags a hard time?'

'No, I never. I wouldn't lie to you, Mum. I'd tell you if I done it, mate, and I did not do it . . . I was always at the beach, not up there. And I wouldn't have done that anyway.'

In another phone conversation, a mate of his says: 'Oh, yeah, I was um, I was talkin' to Jason about that, eh . . . the murders and that. He reckons he knows who did it and that . . . Who do you reckon it'd be?'

'Fuck, I don't know,' replies Cushman.

Hardly clinching or even incriminating evidence concerning the murders at Bondi. The recorded conversations did, however, uncover some shady drug dealings, and further down the track, a number of fresh charges and convictions.

11 SUSPICIOUS MINDS

Steve Page was sitting quietly in his cramped office, surrounded by filing cabinets and a mountain of cardboard boxes, his proof of evidence. After nearly three years of lightning leads, dead ends, high hopes and maddening frustrations, his efforts were finally paying off in an inquest, to begin in a few weeks.

He slouched back in his chair, stony-faced as he stared at the CD tilted between his two palms, reflecting a burst of rainbow colours from the fluorescent light shining down from above. Operation Taradale amounted to 3000 pages of witness testimonies, surveillance and police reports, including a 270-page executive summary that he'd only polished off, after endless drafts, three weeks before. All this—the equivalent of three copies of *War and Peace*—squeezed onto this single sliver of aluminium-coated plastic.

He thought for a moment about the bare minimum he wanted from this investigation. First, that Ross Warren should formally be declared dead, so that his mother could finally achieve the closure she had been denied for over twelve years; second, that John Russell's death should be deemed the result of foul play rather than a drunken accident; third, that Gilles Mattaini, the young man whose disappearance didn't even rate a missing persons report let alone an inquest, should be registered as dead, he too a likely victim of homicide.

Page had set out to give these men what they should have been awarded in the first place: a thorough investigation. Now he dared to think about what other outcomes he wanted for all his hard work: a murder trial leading to convictions. Page knew the inquest would attract a fresh round of publicity to the case, which might open other doors on potential new witnesses. That's why he intended to keep the engine of the investigation humming away as the hearings proceeded.

The Deputy State Coroner, Justice Jacqueline Milledge, would be presiding over the inquest, to open at 9 a.m. on Monday March 31, 2003, to determine whether there was enough evidence from the investigation to turn it into a murder trial. The presumption of innocence in our justice system means that the prosecution must be able to prove enough elements of the crime—beyond reasonable doubt—to create a viable court case. In contrast to the first inquest into John Russell's death, which lasted a paltry 35 minutes back on a chilly July morning in 1990, and Ross Warren's disappearance, which didn't even rate one, this inquest was set to be held over two weeks, with the possibility of it being reconvened later in the year, depending on what emerged in the courtroom.

There was a neat symmetry to Page's first meeting with Milledge at Glebe Coroner's Court nearly eighteen months earlier. He had been standing at the enquiry desk of the court, a grim, grey concrete bunker facing onto traffic-choked Parramatta Road, when Milledge happened to stroll past and overhear him mention the words Operation Taradale to the receptionist. Milledge had heard very good things about this investigation, she complimented him. 'How is it all going?' she asked.

By that stage the basic architecture of the investigation was established, but certain finer points had to be clarified—over surveillance, phone tapping and what would and wouldn't be strong enough to forward as admissible evidence. Page was keen to ask Milledge a few pertinent questions.

She proved helpful and down to earth. A former police constable who went on to study law and become, in relatively quick succession, a magistrate and Deputy State Coroner, Milledge had witnessed first-hand, like Page, some of the worst that society could throw up. Behind her polite demeanour and kindly middle-aged face—one journalist described her as bearing a slight resemblance to Dawn French's vicar of Dibley—Milledge had a mind like a steel trap and a reputation for being a tough-nosed inquisitor. She also had, so Page found, a fine sense of humour.

Milledge inevitably reminded Page of some of the legal swamps he would have to wade through, what witnesses would have to be called forth to sustain the inquiry and what supporting witnesses should have their statements tendered. After a second meeting in her chambers, and another in a conference room with her legal counsel, Page felt Operation Taradale couldn't do much better than with a coroner such as Milledge.

Now here he was with the Taradale disc in his hand, looking back on the long course of the case, pondering his next step, and more broadly, his own future. The moment he realised he was going to quit the police force was when he sat down to write the executive summary of the investigation only six weeks before. In dissecting the case, scrupulously condensing every aspect of it into a clear and digestible form, and finally proofreading it until his eyes glazed over, he began to look back at all the investigations he had worked on, the crooks he had put behind bars, the hard-scrabble moments, the laughs, but in the end, the accumulated stresses over the years. Already he was being sounded out to lead another heavy-duty murder investigation, and all he could think was, *here we go again*.

That's when he realised he had nothing left to give. That he didn't want to spend the rest of his life looking over his shoulder to see if any of the criminals he had put away—and there were enough to fill a small country jail house—were behind him.

The moment of truth really hit while he was in the thick of Operation Taradale. Out of the blue he received a letter from a prisoner warning him that a former cell mate, who had been arrested by Page and was now on parole, had bought a gun and hired a private investigator to find out where he lived. Ever resilient, Page calmly notified his superiors and the crook was duly charged some weeks later with possessing an illegal firearm. He had also been running an amusement park with such reckless abandon that some months earlier a young man had fallen to his death trying to fix a dangerous piece of equipment. Later investigations revealed the ex-crim to be a paedophile.

Although the thug was now safely back behind bars, Page found the whole experience profoundly discomforting, mainly because of the threat to his family. The job had always had its highs and lows, but more and more, the lows seemed to be outweighing the highs. He'd begun suffering from stress-related illnesses—rashes, headaches, shingles, lowered resistance to the flu and infections—common to those in emergency services such as ambulance officers, fire fighters and the military. Everyone has a different-sized glass, so to speak, and Page knew that his was about to overflow.

What struck Page about the list of names on his disk—both the victims and the persons of interest—was how many lived just around the corner from one another in Bondi. John Russell and Craig Jones sank beers in the Bondi Hotel, the same watering hole used by many members of the Bondi Boys; it was conceivable they bought their bread and milk from the same grocery shop, their papers from the same newsagent. 'Rick' worked in a cafe next door to a surf shop where some of the attackers hung out, and lived in a street they frequently sauntered down. Here were neighbours with jarringly different attitudes to life, one a hard-working waiter, struggling to pay his rent on a minimum wage (Rick), living next door to a gang of young men who harboured a seething hatred for the world—one they believed owed them a living.

Page shook his head. If 'Rick' at first seemed a little over-cautious—almost paranoid—in wanting his name suppressed in court and in newspaper stories, maybe it was for good reason. Page leaned over and picked up a hard copy of the investigative summary he had penned, flicking through to the final few paragraphs. This time he wasn't checking for typographical errors or misspellings, but the actual content of his words, staring back at him in black and white:

> I believe that Warren is deceased and I believe it likely that his body entered the water surrounding Marks Park. I believe it likely that the placing of the keys belonging to Warren on the rock shelf may have been done by Warren after being lured to that location, or alternatively, by a finder. I do not believe they were thrown into the position they were found.
>
> I do not believe that Warren or Russell attended Marks Park for the purposes of committing suicide, as both were gay men attending a location that they knew was a gay beat, and were likely there for clandestine sexual encounters. Both Warren and Russell appeared to be in good spirits around the time of the disappearance.
>
> Taking into account violence that was detected at the park against members of the gay community, which includes the [Alan B and 'Rick'] assaults in December 1989 and the homicide of Rattanajurathaporn in July 1990, I believe it is likely that both men met their deaths at that location as a result of the violence.
>
> Examination of available evidence shows that the groups known as the Bondi Boys, the Tamarama Three and the Alexandria Eight were involved in offences of violence targeting members of the gay community in the vicinity of Marks Park at Tamarama.
>
> After examination of all available evidence, I am not able to offer an opinion as to who I believe is likely to be responsible for the deaths of Warren and/or Russell.

Page studied those last lines for just a few seconds. Of course, he did have his strong suspicions. Three sets of suspicions, amounting to five or six names, in fact. But pointing the finger at possible culprits is one thing—providing enough evidence beyond any reasonable doubt quite another. From the very start, he knew this wouldn't be an open-and-shut case.

For over three years now, Page had kept in regular contact with Kay Warren and Ted and Peter Russell, keeping them up to date with developments in the case and informing them of impending press releases so they wouldn't be too upset by stories suddenly popping up in the press. He was equally as open with the families of other gay-bashing murder victims, including the parents and siblings of Richard Johnson and Raymond Keam. He had also contacted the Thai Consulate, formally requesting them to track down the family of Kritchikorn Rattanajurathaporn and inform them of the impending media interest.

Everyone deals with their hurt and grief differently. Kay Warren—whose letters were the catalyst for the investigation—made it clear to Page she wouldn't be attending the inquest. While she was deeply appreciative of his hard work, she explained that she would find the hearings too much of an ordeal, and didn't want to hear any distressing details about her son's murder. She wanted to remember Ross as he was, the loving son who made her laugh, who had made her so proud. Ted and Peter Russell, on the other hand, turned up at the inquest every day, wanting to hear everything, wanting to know as much as possible about the circumstances of their son and brother's death. Two families suspended in grief, but seeking different paths to closure.

Craig Ellis—the only one of Ross's close friends to show at the inquest—made a habit of sitting alone, although he did introduce himself to the Russells. Page had organised for witnesses such as Jacques Musy, who had to work all day, to be driven to and from the Coroner's Court. Sean Cushman, Adam French, Matthew Davis, Sean McAuliffe, David McAuliffe and three other 'persons of interest' were all subpoenaed to give evidence.

Coroner Milledge's forthright style resulted in some charged moments in the courtroom, ones that found their way into the column space and news pages of the Sydney papers. It was her humanity for the victims' families and her refusal to don rose-coloured glasses for the artful dodging of some of the 'persons of interest' that had many in the courtroom silently cheering her on.

As became obvious from police reports and witness testimonies brought before the court, many of the young thugs who were violently assaulting and killing gay men were also regularly bashing their girlfriends. 'There was plenty of violence,' one girlfriend of a Bondi Boy stated in an earlier interview to Page, presented to the court. 'Some of the boys used to beat up their girlfriends all the time.' Among the most aggressive, she attested in a police statement tendered to the court, were ringleader Sean Cushman, who was 'violent all the time', and his mate Timothy Alger.

When 'Rick' was given the witness box, knowing his testimony was critical, he was determined to tell the whole ugly story of the bashing. Wearing charcoal trousers and a white shirt, the compact 168 cm man with the brown, mousy hair leaned towards the legal eagles in front of him and delivered a calm, ten-minute summary of the events of that night. He didn't flinch as he spoke of the initial lacklustre response by the police, didn't bat an eyelid as he described seeing his attackers later in the street. He did, however, give some brief thought to the soothing cigarette he was about to enjoy outside the building.

'My attackers told me that they were going to throw me off where they threw the other guy off,' he declared flatly to the court. 'I think that's what gave me the energy to get away. Otherwise I would have been dead.'

Matthew Davis, one of Kritchikorn Rattanajurathaporn's killers, was among the first persons of interest to take the box. As a teenager, he told the packed courtroom, he was 'filthy on the world'. He described how he was sexually abused as a child by a friend of the family, a paedophile. 'Because I was raped and bashed by this man for years, I thought, okay this bloke was a man, he had sex with another male, so me not having the social skills or the education back then, or the mentality or whatever to differentiate, I couldn't differentiate between paedophilia and homosexuality.'

The net result, he explained, was that he 'hated [homosexuals] with a passion'.

Davis candidly admitted: 'Basically what it was with me was that I was a victim for years. Then one day, you're a teenager and the hormones kick in, you fill out a bit, you grow up and—sorry about the language—you say to yourself, "fuck this, I am never going to be a victim again. No-one is ever gonna hurt me again."'

Davis hastened to add that his mind-set changed as he got older.

'When you mature you get compassion; you realise paedophiles are not homosexuals.' He made friends with some gay men in prison, he explained, and realised 'that it's not gay people who, you know, do that, it's paedophiles'.

He added: 'I dealt with that [the sexual abuse] while I was in prison with psychs and stuff . . . now I realise I could have dealt with this stuff earlier, I could have prevented the last twelve years being lost, you know.'

Davis said he had no knowledge of what happened to Mr Russell, Mr Warren or Mr Mattaini. 'I admit I was an angry young man but I did not do it,' he said. 'I will even take a polygraph test.'

After the session, Davis, who had spent twelve years in jail for killing Rattanajurathaporn, shook the hands of Ted and Peter Russell, who were seated in the front row of the courtroom, designated for family members. 'I had nothing to do with your brother and your son's death,' he told them, as he was about to leave. 'I hope you get closure.'

Ted and Peter Russell nodded and shook Davis's hand, but if they seemed like they were in a forgiving mood, they were not. They had a strong suspicion that the man or men who had slaughtered their son and brother would be walking in and out of this courtroom in the next few weeks, if they hadn't done so already. If nothing else, they were at least face to face with some of the young men who thought it a sport to destroy lives.

While Davis's compelling claim to the police that Cushman and one of the McAuliffe brothers had bashed and thrown a man off the cliff fit the timeframe and modus operandi of the murders perfectly, it bore little weight without independent corroboration, at least as far as the courts were concerned. Page also knew that Davis was implicating the McAuliffes and Cushman at the precise time he was likely to be going back into jail himself, and may have wanted to curry favour with the police. By this stage, too, Cushman's name had appeared in the papers, so it was conceivable Davis had plucked it from there. All of which, of course, didn't discount the potential truth of his story.

But if Davis appeared genuinely regretful to the court about his earlier history of violence, it didn't last for very long. Only a few months later, he was wanted for the attempted murder of his girlfriend, who was at the police station when Page was taking Davis's statement for the inquest. Page remembered her as a nice, quiet girl in her late twenties who said she was there to give Matthew support. Davis—now in his early thirties—later told witnesses he 'red rummed' her, using the street slang/word reversal of his youth, as in gaf/fag, redrum/murder.

Also present and handcuffed during the first week of the inquest were brothers Sean and David McAuliffe, still serving out their sentences for the murder of Kritchikorn Rattanajurathaporn. They, too, denied any involvement in the earlier deaths of John Russell (six months before) or Ross Warren (twelve months earlier).

As the lawyers, witnesses and journalists milled about the lobby during a mid-morning break, Steve Page was reminded that identifying possible culprits might be the easy part; bringing enough evidence to turn the inquest into a murder investigation quite another. Providing evidence beyond any reasonable doubt was the biggest challenge for any detective—and especially challenging in a case like this.

If the testimonies of former gang members proved hard to listen to, playing the 1991 surveillance tapes proved excruciating, particularly for the friends of Ross Warren and the family of John Russell. The courtroom heard some chilling interchanges, such as this one between Bradley Young, Dean Howard and others.

'I used to go fishing at Bondi.'

'Yeah, fishing for poofters in the area. Fuckin' use 'em as bait, throw the c∗∗∗s off the cliff.'

And another one from 1991: 'I threw a fag off the cliff at Bondi. I've jumped on blokes' heads you wouldn't believe it; we were always going out bashing fags . . .'

The words, which reflected a cruelty and absence of conscience most people in the courtroom could barely comprehend, left a vivid gash in the minds of Ted and Peter Russell. They knew the words 'threw a fag off the cliff at Bondi' could easily refer to their much-loved son and brother John.

For a while they were too shaken to speak. 'At some stage, John's killer is probably going to walk through the courtroom,' Ted later told me over a sandwich and coffee during a break in the proceedings. That some of these young men were but teenage boys at the time did nothing to assuage his anger. 'It doesn't matter that they were just teenage boys. Their age doesn't change the fact they murdered my son. Kids do things on the spur of the moment. What these boys did was not on the spur of the moment.'

There is a truth in Ted Russell's words. The modern murder charge rests on a concept called 'malice aforethought': a person goes out and deliberately kills another intentionally, understands his actions and dismisses the voices, if any, of his conscience. Warren, Russell and Rattanajurathaporn were not victims of a random, spontaneous act of violence, but rather a premeditated hate crime. What defined their deaths was that they were murdered for *what* they were, not *who* they were.

For Ted, the prospect that his son's lonely, horrific death might wind up a crime without punishment was too difficult to bear. But he knew Page had made a sterling effort with his investigation, and this was his best chance yet of seeing some form of justice done.

Transcripts of various bugged conversations—both in 1991 and 2001—revealed to the court just how deep the fear and loathing of gays was among these young men. When asked why he 'bashed fags' one assailant spat, 'Oh it's a fuckin' hobby, mate. What are you doin' tonight boys? Oh, just going fag bashin'.'

Further accounts of assaults on gay men, read to the court, included: 'Them c∗∗∗s copped a bad hiding, two of 'em did anyway. We were jumping off the roof of his car onto his head, mate. His head was on the gutter . . .'

With evidence such as this being rolled out, one would have to be remarkably soft-headed to believe the steady stream of denials from former gang members summoned to the witness stand. No, they had never been to Marks Park, they claimed. No, they had nothing to do with, or had any knowledge of, the deaths of Ross Warren and John Russell. Some even claimed they 'didn't have a problem' with gay men at the time.

Sue Thompson, who had given Page such invaluable assistance in assembling his list of gay hate crimes, but who had now quit her post as NSW Gay and Lesbian Liaison Officer, explained to the court how gay bashing was a recreational pastime for these gangs. The auburn-haired, slim thirtysomething explained to the court how one gang member boasted to police that they 'thought it was a great way to spend their time . . . go gay bashing it used to be called'.

Thompson described how, in the aftermath of Richard Johnson's murder, she conducted training days on homophobia to selected secondary schools such as Cleveland Street Boys High. This had a surprising dual benefit, she explained. It not only educated students in the art of tolerating 'differences' in others, it also provided feedback to the police on school-based gangs and likely troublemakers. Sadly, the impetus for these homophobia workshops—and gay and lesbian liaison officers—had been lost in recent years, she added.

Kenneth Bowditch, chief of detectives at Bondi Police Station at the time Ross Warren disappeared, next appeared to give evidence.

In a sworn statement to police in 2001, Bowditch, who has since left the police force, said the following:

> There is nothing to suggest that Ross Warren's disappearance was the result of foul play or a deliberate ploy on his part to disappear . . .
>
> There is a distinct possibility that Ross Warren may have slipped on the rock ledge overlooking Mackenzies Bay. It was not unusual and is still not unusual to see people sitting on the rocks day or night. I inspected the scene during the initial investigation and I am extremely familiar with the area as I regularly walk between Bondi and Bronte.

It was a view he doggedly adhered to throughout the inquest. He conceded that he knew of Marks Park's reputation and was aware that the media of the time were claiming Ross Warren's death was suspicious. But he did not believe the television presenter had been murdered and insisted he'd made every effort to get to the bottom of his disappearance.

Bowditch claimed that he had prepared a brief for the coroner, which was also sent to the Missing Persons Unit. He insisted that 'reams and reams' of paperwork would have been produced, 'but where that documentation is, I don't know'.

When confronted with the lack of basic police procedures in the case, such as crime scene photographs, fingerprint dusting of Warren's car, and doorknocks in the vicinity, Bowditch became flustered and angry.

'I will not be a scapegoat for the inadequacies of the department,' he thundered, 'which was responsible for losing all the records.' He also denied the complaints by gay witnesses that they had been 'fobbed off', insisting that 'extreme effort' had been made to deal with the local gay community. But when pressed on what this 'extreme effort' amounted to, Bowditch couldn't or wouldn't elaborate.

Coroner Milledge was not mollified. Her counsel, Paul Lakatos, said the occurrence page written by Bowditch nominated three officers assigned to the Warren investigation, but upon further crosschecks, all confirmed they were on other duties at the time. One was on annual leave.

Sally Dunbar had been a police detective for just four years when she was put in charge of the investigation into John Russell's death. She told coroner Milledge she could recall the clumps of hair behind Mr Russell's index finger, was certain they were bagged but had no idea what happened to them once they left the crime scene. Dunbar couldn't remember why she hadn't chased up the results from this crucial piece of evidence, which would have revealed they'd been lost.

Ted Russell was horrified as he listened to Dunbar's testimony. He knew that if the evidence hadn't been lost, it's highly likely that the police would have known straightaway that John had been murdered.

If the memories of some police officers were proving a little soft around the edges, those of former gang members were especially fuzzy. Sean Cushman, sporting a flat-top haircut, a white open-necked shirt and jeans, denied being a member of any gang that violently targeted gay men. 'We grew up in Bondi; that's why we called ourselves the Bondi Boys,' he said. 'I was never in a gang or crew. We didn't roll homosexuals.'

Cushman admitted he was a member of a group that regularly met near the Bondi Pavilion and hung out at the beach. But they didn't assault people or attack gay men, he claimed.

Pulling on a grey hooded sweatshirt that he had been carrying, Cushman seemed very keen to keep his face hidden from the prying lenses of newspaper photographers and television cameras as he strode into, and exited, the building. He waved one persistent photographer from *The Sydney Morning Herald* away, his face obscured by the grey hood and a pair of dark rectangular glasses. The gangly blond was at one point seen clenching and unclenching his fists outside the courtroom.

All quite a departure from the man who in 1999 gave waiting photographers a broad, smug smile after being acquitted of being an accessory after the fact in the murder of Brian Hagland. A year before his appearance at the inquest, Cushman had been arrested and convicted of drug charges as a result of the phone tapping and surveillance of Operation Taradale. But he was already back on the streets, having served less than twelve months in prison.

If the now 30-year-old Cushman did have a story to tell to the court, he wasn't willing to share it, and not just on the matter of what he got up to in Bondi in the late 1980s.

If he was going to share his story, it might have begun with the biographical basics, how he was born in Vancouver, Canada, in June 1973, how he went to Dover Heights High School, how he has two children, a boy and a girl, by his ex de facto, how he has been unable to last in a job—as a labourer, tree lopper—for more than a couple of months, how he has never held a driver's licence, even though he has owned (or illegally driven) at least eight cars. He might pull up his shirt sleeves and show the court his tattoos—a Celtic band on his right bicep, a dragon on his left—and describe how he had his appendix out while he was still in primary school, which left him with a 100 mm scar on his stomach.

Cushman might then move on to the recurrent theme of his life, a roiling anger that when fuelled with alcohol and drugs, burst into violent relief. He might describe how he casually stood by while his mate brutally bashed an innocent British tourist to death, and how he convinced the jury of his contrition, only to gloat to a woman a year afterwards how he killed a man and got away with it. He might recall the time at the North Bondi

RSL in 1998, when he became so abusive towards bar staff, tossing furniture about, that the RSL's director marched down to the floor to ask him to leave. He might chuckle to himself as he described how, after apologising to the manager and shaking his hand, he coldly threatened him with: 'I know where you live and I know what car you drive.' He might think it even funnier that when the manager returned to his vehicle in the car park ten minutes later, a thick wad of burning newspaper was protruding from the petrol tank, which resulted in the fire brigade being called in and the club evacuated. He might wrap up that particular story by relaying how the manager's car, in addition to some minor fire damage, had been smothered in scratches, probably from a key.

But if Cushman was really going to open up to the court—and in the process perhaps gain some sympathy for his own story of hardship—he might tell them about growing up in a broken home, his disorganised, undisciplined childhood, hanging out with street kids by the age of 12, and being a constant troublemaker at Dover Heights High (when he deigned to turn up to school).

Of course, none of this answers the central question: did Sean Cushman have anything to do with, or any knowledge of, the murders at Bondi? 'Rick' identified him as the ringleader of the group who bashed and dragged him to the edge of the cliff tops in December 1989; Cushman was allegedly involved in other gay bashings during the period that Ross Warren and John Russell met their demise. At the very least, surely he knew something?

No, he hadn't heard of John Russell, he claimed, and he only knew Ross Warren's name from the newspapers.

Like other 'persons of interest', barman Justin King had no idea why he had been identified as the perpetrator of 'the most gay bashings' in a 1991 bugged conversation between Adam French and Dean Howard, convicted for their part in the murder of Richard Johnson at Alexandria Park. He claimed he had never been involved in any gay bashings.

Patrick Saidi, counsel for the Police Commissioner, accused King of mixing with a gay-hate gang, which King denied.

'You are completely misleading this inquest, aren't you?' Saidi snapped, looking King directly in the eye.

'No . . . I'm not,' King muttered, glancing away.

Former footballer Darrell Trindall managed to avoid the inquest witness box altogether. A prepared statement from his lawyer was read to the court, in which he denied any involvement with gay-hate gangs. Steve Page explained that while Trindall wasn't a person of interest in relation to the deaths of Warren and Russell, he was a member of a gay-bashing gang that prowled Centennial Park. He stood in the witness box and read out Adam French's words from the tape recording of July 7, 1991. 'We went there heaps of times . . . to Centennial . . . you were there when we got the guy with the wig, there was Trindall, me, Sharkey and Brad.'

The words, 'they'd belted him at Moore Park . . . and took his wig. Trindall pissed in it and they chucked it in a hollow tree,' reverberated throughout the courtroom.

At the time of the inquest, Trindall, who had a long history of charges for assault and drink driving, was again before the courts for groping a woman's breasts and punching her in the face after she spurned his advances in a nightclub. The woman, Kelly Robb, who had known Trindall for eighteen years, claimed he put her in a headlock and slammed her against a wall.

Trindall, the court was told, laughed off her threats to call the police, yelling: 'I am a first-grade footballer [he was then playing for the Canterbury Bulldogs in Sydney]. Who are they going to believe, you or me?'

Later in the year Trindall, already on a suspended jail sentence for the assault on Robb, was again before the courts, this time for threatening to rape and kill an ex-girlfriend. All of which didn't stop Sydney radio announcer Alan Jones—a closet homosexual and the subject of a recent biography by ABC journalist Chris Masters—from attending Trindall's wedding, helping him with investment and career opportunities, and using his powerful contacts to help get him out of strife with the police.

As Peter Russell listened to more and more evidence being tendered, and more and more persons of interest denying any involvement in anti-gay violence, he became resigned to the fact that the case might never be solved. 'If the police had done their jobs properly back in '89 we wouldn't be sitting here now,' he said. 'We wouldn't be sitting in front of an inquiry and reliving the nightmare.'

In the course of the inquest, which reconvened in September 2003, it was noted to the court that the attacks on 'Rick', John Russell and Richard Johnson all shared the same timeframe—occurring in the summer months between late November 1989 and late January 1990. Ross Warren's disappearance occurred six months earlier, in winter, perhaps suggesting that a different set of killers may have been responsible. Then again,

Kritchikorn Rattanajurathaporn was also murdered in July, one day from the anniversary of the newsreader's death.

But who, then, killed Gilles Mattaini, if indeed he was murdered? Was this a warm-up to the other murders? Page made it clear to the court that he doubted Gilles's death was linked to the others, although he didn't rule out the possibility of an earlier, older gang of killers sharing loose connections—or perhaps gruesome strategies—with the gangs who murdered John Russell and Ross Warren.

What made this investigation especially complicated, he told the court, was that there were several knots of suspects—some likely murderers, some not—and there wasn't enough evidence to charge any single individual. Anti-gay hate gangs were all over Sydney at the time.

'With a traditional homicide you study the victim, look at potential motives, identify suspects from those motives and close in,' he told this writer during the inquest. 'With generic hatred (as opposed to specific motive) the crime is more random and harder to solve. That no doubt explains why some police missed it. A lot of the crimes passed off as isolated suicides or disappearances at the time were in fact gay hate crimes.'

If there was one issue all parties agreed on it was that beats are dangerous places, and any man who visits them is risking life and limb. One witness, a gay man, declared to the court:

> My philosophy is very simple. A lot of gay guys don't agree with me but I believe it's all over, red rover. You know the days of going and doing beats, searching for partners, is dangerous, risky business and I'm not saying that people who go there deserve any sort of retaliation but I'm saying

we need to take responsibility for our own behaviour and I think the message needs to go out loud ... in the gay community, which I am a part of. I believe that we need to look at these things and say okay these are the problems, right, we shouldn't be going down to these parks because they are too dangerous.

After the inquest folded in late September 2003, everyone from Steve Page to former gang members to the victims' families had to play a waiting game.

One that revolved around a single individual: Deputy State Coroner Jacqueline Milledge.

12   END GAME

May 2005

Finally. Five years to the month after Steve Page first opened Kay Warren's letters with their pleas for some kind of closure on her son's death, Deputy State Coroner Jacqueline Milledge was due to bring down her findings and recommendations on the Taradale investigation. Milledge had listened to the harrowing details of the violent assaults and murders on the Bondi cliff tops, she had watched the effects of this testimony on the friends and families of Ross Warren, John Russell and Gilles Mattaini, and she had spent months patiently combing through and assessing more than 3000 pages of investigative notes.

Winter seemed to be coming fast on this brisk morning in early May, 2005. You could feel it in the air as large ships of clouds sailed slowly across the blue sky, and a crisp breeze cleared up much of Parramatta Road's regular haze of carbon monoxide. By now, Steve Page had been out of the force for over six months, had set up a lawnmowing business on Sydney's leafy North Shore and was looking around at senior security positions as well. But there was no way he was going to miss hearing Milledge's findings. Dressed in a dark suit with a white shirt and blue tie, he turned up at the Coroner's Court about fifteen minutes early, chatting briefly to Craig Ellis and some familiar faces among the press contingent.

One of the ironies was that at this, the climax of the proceedings, the courtroom was half deserted. The earlier hearings in 2003, by contrast, had usually been jammed with the families and friends of the victims, journalists, witnesses and interested spectators. This time there were no family members, and only a few friends of the deceased, but the media were out in force, with journalists from *The Australian, The Sydney Morning Herald,* the *Illawarra Mercury* and gay papers such as the *Sydney Star Observer* seated in the press gallery along the right-hand side of the courtroom. Two or three television camera crews—forbidden from entering the courtroom—hovered outside.

It had been a marathon three-year investigation, followed by an inquest broken into two sessions over eighteen long months, so if the proceedings had an air of world-weariness about them, it was understandable. The formidable Milledge, however, no sooner sat down than she snapped the entire courtroom to attention, hurling one verbal thunderbolt after another against the 1989 investigations into the deaths of Warren and Russell, which she labelled 'grossly inadequate and shameful'.

As press journalists frantically scribbled shorthand into their notepads, Milledge delivered a blistering broadside aimed at the Bondi police in the late 1980s:

The disappearance of Ross Bradley Warren was reported to police within 48 hours of his last sighting. The investigation was coordinated by Detective Sergeant Bowditch; however within the week he had effectively 'closed' any further investigation by concluding Mr Warren dead by misadventure.

He was insistent that his brief of evidence was submitted to the coroner in 1990. No brief of evidence was ever received by this office.

He stated copies of all documents would have been sent to Missing Persons to be kept in a folder. There are no photographs of Mr Warren's car, keys or crime scene.

He assured the inquest that the Scientific Section, the Air Wing and the Water Police were called to examine the area. There were no records of any of the specialist police having been 'activated'.

He nominated three other officers as assisting him in the investigation. Two of those officers deny any involvement in the investigation, the third was on annual leave at the time of being nominated.

This state of affairs defies belief. This was a grossly inadequate investigation. Indeed to characterise it as an 'investigation' is to give it a label it does not deserve. Bowditch knew that the area was a 'gay beat' . . . however, he paid little or no regard to the possibility of foul play.

Milledge acknowledged that a 'better' investigation was performed into John Russell's death, but it too was 'far from adequate'. The disappearance of Warren only six months earlier should have put the police on the scent, she argued.

Had police paid careful attention to [John Russell's] crime scene and the vital evidence presented to them, the perpetrator of that brutal act may have been identified or, at the very least, Mr Russell's death would have been differently and not simply as a result of 'misadventure'.

Unlike the Warren case, good crime scene photos were taken of Mr Russell's body and surroundings. In a number of the photos a clump of hair can be seen in his hand.

Whilst evidence was given that those vital hairs were secured and bagged for forensic testing, none was undertaken and the exhibit was lost.

Disgraceful!

The police officers that should have been responsible for the safe storage of exhibits blamed each other for its disappearance by stating the other should have been responsible for its safe keeping.

Not good enough!

Unfortunately the significance of [the hair] appears to have been lost on the police officers. Like the missing Warren brief of evidence, this important exhibit has never been found nor has a satisfactory explanation been given as to the reason it was not safeguarded at the time.

The positioning of Mr Russell's body should also have triggered some concerns for the investigating officers.

In both Mr Warren's disappearance and Mr Russell's death there were similarities that should have linked them in the early stages of the investigation and suggested to the police the possibility of foul play in both deaths.

Both men were homosexual. The last place either man was prior to death was Marks Park. Mr Russell had coins scattered near his body, Mr Warren's keys were found on the rocks. This was a known area for brutal attacks on homosexual males. Yet investigating police believed Mr Warren and Mr Russell met their death by 'misadventure'.

If the earlier investigations were 'inadequate and naive', Milledge hailed Page's Operation Taradale as 'a shining example of how investigations should be conducted and the sensitivity and compassion that is often needed when dealing with persons who have been marginalised'.

The inquest was hampered, she complained, by the wall of obstruction set up by former gang members of the Bondi Boys, the Alexandria Eight and the Tamarama Three. That virtually all of them denied committing even one act of general violence against homosexual men was not only implausible but cast a deep pall of suspicion over their steady stream of denials. 'The evidence they gave was completely at odds with the police intelligence gathered during the course of the investigation,' she declared.

Milledge suspected that some of the men responsible for the deaths of Ross Warren and John Russell had passed through the courtroom. 'A number of witnesses are in custody, serving sentences for similar matters being considered by this inquest,' she noted, referring to the murder of other gay men in Sydney's eastern suburbs. 'It was quite possible,' she added, 'they were involved in other murders as well.'

Never one to skate past the ugly, unpleasant details of a case, Milledge read out excerpts from some of the sinister bugged conversations, in which gang members gloated about smashing heads and breaking arms. Nor did she blanch as she read out words like 'cunt', 'fuck', 'fag' and 'gaf' to the courtroom. 'These brutes who prey on people are cowardly and boastful,' she declared.

A sense of expectation surged through the courtroom as Milledge gradually pulled back the curtain on her findings. She reminded the press gallery that transcripts of what she was about to say would be available at the end of the session.

She paused for a moment, put one hand over the other and declared:

> I am comfortably satisfied that I can make the finding of 'foul' play in relation to Mr Warren and Mr Russell, but I cannot make a finding that Mr Mattaini met his death at the hands of another person or persons. The persons of interest that may have been responsible for the deaths of Mr Warren and Mr Russell would have been far too young at the time of Mr Mattaini's disappearance in September 1985.
>
> I can, however, bring a finding of 'death', but where and how he died remains unknown, although there is a strong possibility that he died in similar circumstances to the other men.

So far, so good. In dissecting the case, Milledge strongly believed that the weight of evidence clearly pointed to Ross Warren and John Russell having been murdered, and that Mattaini's death was suspicious. That much was now official. But taking the evidence one step further—laying charges and turning these into murder trials—was the more challenging part of the equation. The problem, she explained, was that there was 'insufficient evidence to make a finding against any one person'. It was hard to tangibly demonstrate that one particular individual or group was responsible for either of the Bondi killings.

But what of the damning disclosures from the tape recordings of 1991, which clearly seemed to point to victims being pushed over the cliff edge at Bondi? It might sound persuasive, Milledge concluded, and 'whilst a layperson could get quite excited about hearing one of them boast they had some involvement in the [Bondi deaths], without any independent evidence linking them to the event they could not be prosecuted successfully for any crime'.

Milledge knew this would be a disappointing result—terribly so—for many in the courtroom. It certainly wasn't the golden finish Page had hoped for when he began his investigation. She reflected that the real killers might now be safely behind bars if the original investigations into the deaths of Russell and Warren had been undertaken competently.

But she also noted that as a side effect of Page's 'first class' investigation, fourteen men had been arrested on multiple drugs charges, including supply and possession of ecstasy and methamphetamines. (One of the charged, Sean Cushman, was already out on parole by the time Milledge was drafting her recommendations. Rumours were swirling that he had fled to Byron Bay in fear of his life, having had a major falling out with his old mate Aaron Martin over a botched drug deal.)

But it's not over yet, Milledge suggested.

> The wealth of evidence gathered by Detective Page and his team, however, will provide an excellent source of evidence should other matters come to light. It is always possible that someone will decide to tell police what they know about a perpetrator if they feel the need. Relationships between these thugs do not always remain 'solid'.

Milledge leaned forward and looked in the direction of where Page was sitting. 'I don't think anyone will ever follow in your footsteps. Your conduct and professionalism are unsurpassed. You stand alone.'

As in the earlier sessions of the inquest, Milledge made a point of not naming civilian witnesses—some of them traumatised victims—in her findings. She commended their courage in coming forward to tell their stories. Of the victims themselves—John Russell, Ross Warren and Gilles Mattaini—Milledge said movingly: 'It's important we do the best by these men, for they were loved and they were decent men.'

The traditional reluctance of some gay men to come forward and report crimes committed against them was something the police had to address, Milledge suggested.

> Given the disgraceful investigation into Mr Warren's suspected death and the completely 'lacklustre' investigation into Mr Russell's demise, it would not be unreasonable for the gay community to believe that as a group they do not warrant proper police attention. It is hard for the NSW Police Force to be seen as progressive and equitable when some officers fail in their duty to the community they are meant to serve. With all good intentions many police officers are trying to do their best with limited education on how to deal with the problem.
>
> I cannot make recommendations to change community attitudes towards homosexuals or for homosexuals to abandon the use of 'beats'. All I can do is urge communities, through my finding, to regard any victimisation of a gay man or lesbian as completely abhorrent and not to be tolerated.

Hindsight is 20/20, of course. But once in a while foresight is too. Milledge made twelve major recommendations to the Minister of Police and the Police Commissioner—recommendations that, if carried into policy, will make the lives of all victims of crime easier. Among them were ensuring that 'missing person' cases considered suspicious deaths be referred for criminal investigation, that procedures for the collection of physical evidence relating to unsolved homicides be reviewed, and to reintroduce the gay liaison officers program.

◆

Outside the Coroner's Court, Page was faced with a phalanx of television cameras and radio microphones, all trying to grab a sound bite. 'I'm extremely pleased with the findings, and also the opinions the Coroner expressed,' he said. 'But the job isn't over. The police department will keep digging.'

When I asked him to explain his principal motive in pursuing the investigation, he replied: 'I wanted to look the parents of these men in the eye, knowing I had done all that was possible.' That unwavering goal, which he had set himself five years earlier, was now at least complete.

Although it wasn't quite the result he'd hoped for, Page took some comfort from the fact that he'd pinned fourteen men—four of them 'persons of interest'—on lesser charges such as drug trafficking. 'I would have liked to have finalised this with a couple of homicide prosecutions, but at least most of them are off the streets—for the time being,' he told me. 'After all, they couldn't pin Al Capone as a gangster, but they finally got him on tax evasion.'

Modest and circumspect to a fault, Page would never use the words 'sloppy' or 'grossly unprofessional' to describe the initial police response to the deaths of Warren and Russell—such words were left for Coroner Milledge, always one to call a spade a spade. Nonetheless, Page candidly admitted that morning: 'I think if the police had managed it a lot better back then [in 1989], we wouldn't have been giving evidence before a coroner over fifteen years later. It would have been before a jury and we would have had true finalisation for the families.'

Later that day, on ABC radio's 'PM' program, reporter David Mark asked Page: 'Do you believe there will come a time when people are prosecuted for these crimes?'

'It's not beyond the realms of possibility,' he replied. 'I've been involved in matters before which have been cold for many, many years, and then all of a sudden a witness comes out of the blue and we can just keep our fingers crossed.'

That night Steve Page drove home with a clear mind. The next day, in the warm sunshine of a perfect autumn day, he was busy mowing lawns in Chatswood, soaking in the fresh air, smelling his cut grass—and revelling in the fact that he was no longer under the gun, hunting down murderers and thugs.

◆

Page may not have realised it when he began ferreting through old police reports in 2000, but Operation Taradale turned out to be the most intensive investigation into gay hate crimes ever conducted in Australia. In peeling back the layers of a concerted anti-gay crime wave in the late 1980s and early 1990s, he revealed how easily and swiftly anti-gay prejudice can morph into violence and murder.

Because of police indifference and inaction, gangs of young men were able to roam the Bondi cliff tops in the late 1980s with virtual impunity, bashing and killing people at will, with little fear of the long arm of the law catching up with them. In a very real sense, Ross Warren, John Russell and Gilles Mattaini never had a hope, not in the last minutes of their lives, not in the investigations that immediately followed their deaths.

If Operation Taradale revealed the evil senselessness of their deaths, it also—amid the fog of conflicting and compelling reports—raised new mysteries. Was the same group of killers responsible for the deaths of both Warren and Russell? If not, did they know one another? Did John Russell, in the final moments of his life, deliberately try to leave some vital clues in his hand by clutching his killer's hair? Did their killers ever confess their dark deeds to others, who to this day are harbouring their awful secret?

When Page launched his investigation, he was seeking posthumous justice for the victims' ghosts—and some degree of closure for their families. This he accomplished with enormous professional aplomb, providing these murdered men with the investigation long overdue them.

But the ghosts of Russell and Warren aren't quite settled yet.

◆

Sinking back in his plush leather sofa, looking out over the neon lights of Kings Cross on a thundery evening in May 2005, only weeks after Coroner Milledge had brought down her findings, Craig Ellis was reflecting on the events of the night of July 21, 1989. Ross's arrival at his house in Redfern. The laughs over pizza. The little bits of paper strewn over his dining table. His final sight of Ross disappearing down his hallway. The clap of the front door slamming shut behind him. The keys in the rock face. The hot, sad tears of Ross's mother.

As the blinding rain lashed against the sliding glass doors of his balcony, the now 38-year-old Ellis—tall and marine-handsome with a new buzz cut—sipped from his beer. 'Ross would be in his early forties now; who knows what he could have achieved,' he told me. 'The way he was going in his career, he could easily have become a household name. Or at least a major TV identity. I still remember those piercing pale blue eyes, that olive skin, the sound of his laughter.'

The media circus surrounding his disappearance was particularly painful, Ellis recalled. 'The poor guy, the way certain sections of the media portrayed it, Ross was to blame himself, you know, for being a promiscuous gay. But he wasn't especially promiscuous—well, at least not by the standards of most 25-year-olds—he didn't take party drugs, and he wasn't a big rager.

'For a very long time after his disappearance, I really missed having him about. But it's his family that I still think about—being left with all those unanswered questions.'

He's not the only one, of course. Some months after the conversation with Craig Ellis, near the twentieth anniversary of Gilles Mattaini's disappearance, I met Jacques Musy in a cafe near Sydney's Town Hall station. The now 55-year-old brought some photos of their shared youthful life together: happy snaps on the golden sands of Bali, the cobbled streets of Paris, relaxing in their Bondi flat.

Though much of his loss is now anchored in these now fading photos—all taken between 1978 and

1985—he still thinks about Gilles most days, he says. And in the quiet hours, after a long day spent working in a bank in Sydney's CBD, he still occasionally sinks into a mood of sorrow and longing. 'It's a hole and it doesn't go away,' he said, patting his grey thinning hair. 'I really did think we would be spending our lives together.'

Some months afterwards, Jacques returned to France for good, having spent more than 23 years in Australia, virtually all of it in Bondi. His elderly mother had fallen ill, and being an only child he had no choice but to return to his homeland. As he packed up his things, he came across the 1985 Ken Done calendar with Gilles's handwriting on it. 'Life is so short, and when you have a good relationship, you want it to last as long as possible,' he told me, cradling the calendar in his hands. 'He was taken away from me suddenly, and I never got a chance to say the things I wanted. Such as thank you for all the happiness you brought me. I love you. And of course, goodbye . . .'

Twelve months after Jacqueline Milledge gave Steve Page one of the most glowing reports ever handed out by a coroner to a detective in Australia, a commendation from the police department finally lobbed in his letterbox.

'It gives me a sense of completion,' he said. 'But a case like this never really closes when their killers are still out there.'

Of one thing Page is sure. The past of these killers will pursue them, until the day they die.

EPILOGUE: TOWARDS THE ROOT OF THE EVIL

It's important we do the very best for these men, for they were loved, and they were decent men.
　　　　　　　　　NSW Deputy State Coroner,
　　　　　　　　　　　　Jacqueline Milledge

Three gay men murdered on the Bondi cliff tops. Five others slaughtered in the inner city, all in the same two-year timeframe. Dozens of relatives and friends left to grieve. Questions that have been unanswered for over seventeen years. Questions that may indeed never be answered, even if some of the killers are found.

We can be sure of one thing, however. Ross Warren and John Russell were lynched on the cliff tops of Bondi to make a point: We hate faggots and they don't deserve to live. We can bash the crap out of them and they won't stand a chance. Not on their own. Not against the ten of us. 'Why be a fuckin' poofter?' the ringleader of the Bondi Boys growled at 'Rick' as he kicked and punched him.

As we have seen, one of the trademarks of a hate crime is its relentless, cold-blooded cruelty, the sheer pleasure an attacker draws from seeing his victim squirm and beg for mercy. If robbery happens, it's almost an afterthought, the mere icing on the cake. 'Used to love how they scream,' one gay-basher boasted in a police statement. 'I was gunna hit him again . . . "ah, help, help" . . . heaps funny.'

Australians don't hold an exclusive licence on homophobia, of course. Surveys consistently show that we are among the most tolerant societies on the planet. The sad truth is that homophobia—like racism—has ancient and deep roots, from the time of the Bible to Hitler's gas chambers, into which the men with pink triangles were herded shoulder to shoulder with the Jews. Fundamentalist Christians and Muslims continue to make life a misery for gay men, whether it be in the so-called 'conversion' camps of the United States, where desperate, self-loathing homosexuals are supposedly 'cured' by counselling sessions that include smashing tennis racquets against pillows, to the jails of the Middle East, where gay men are routinely incarcerated.

Jamaica now has the dubious honour of being the gay-murder capital of the world, spurred on by local artists like Beanie Man, one of the world's biggest reggae stars, who advocates that gay people be shot, drowned, hanged or stamped to death. Beanie Man's fellow Jamaican reggae artists, Sizzla, Bounty Killer and Elephant Man proclaim that gay men should be set ablaze and macheted. 'Queers are to be killed/Give me the Tech-9 [machine gun]/Shoot them like birds,' Elephant Man proclaims in 'We Nuh Like Gay'. Murder music is what they call it, and it took fierce lobbying from Britain's gay community in 2004 to prevent Sizzla from touring.

It's no accident that homosexuals are persecuted most in countries where women, too, are oppressed, as the gay rights movement in Western countries grew directly out of women's liberation in the 1960s. Thus Saudi Arabia, where women are not allowed to drive a car or walk down the street unescorted by a male relative, has one of the most dismal records on human rights for homosexuals.

Even in the United States, home of the television comedy *Will & Grace* and an Oscar-winning gay cowboy movie, sodomy is still a crime in thirteen states, and it's conservatively estimated that one gay man a week is murdered. On a freezing October night in 1998, on the outskirts of the town of Laramie in Wyoming, a 21-year-old gay college student called Matthew Shepard was savagely beaten, tied to a fence and left for dead. At least eighteen blows from fists and the butt of a handgun had crushed his head. He was left lying on his back, his hands bound beneath him, his ankles tied with a clothes line. From the roadside all that could be seen of the 162 cm, 55 kg undergraduate were his feet, poking out of a sage bush.

It was eighteen hours before a cyclist found Shepard, at first mistaking him for a scarecrow. After he was rushed to hospital, Shepard lingered on the edge of death for nearly five days before succumbing to his injuries. News of his horrifying murder sparked reaction overseas and demonstrations across America. But if Shepard became a martyr for gay rights, his death also triggered a corresponding backlash from anti-gay opponents eager to grab a share of the media spotlight. Tensions were so high that Shepard's father wore a bulletproof vest under his suit when he spoke at his son's funeral, which was picketed by fundamentalist Christians carrying placards such as 'God Hates Fags'.

In a highly publicised television interview in 2004, Shepard's killers claimed that it was money and drugs that motivated their actions that night, not hatred of gays. But the court transcripts tell a different story—of the duo pretending they were gay, of luring Shepard out of a downtown bar, of abusing him again and again as a faggot, of beating him into unconsciousness. In short, not such a different modus operandi from the gay-bashers on the Bondi cliff tops, who drew their many victims into the bushes, or down to the rock platform below, before attacking them with fists, boots, claw hammers, whatever crude instrument came to hand.

What, then, turns young men into the murderers of gay men? Both Aaron McKinney and Russell Henderson, Shepard's killers, came from classically troubled backgrounds. Henderson was born to a teenage alcoholic and raised without a father; McKinney's father, a long-haul trucker, was rarely home and eventually divorced McKinney's mother, a nurse who later died from a botched operation. But there are plenty of young men who have survived far greater traumas than these and haven't proceeded to take out all their bitterness and rage on homosexuals.

Thus the pop-psych explanation—that those who commit violent offences against gay men must have suffered sexual or physical abuse themselves—doesn't necessarily hold up to close scrutiny. Certainly, some members of the Bondi Boys and the Alexandria Eight came from disturbed backgrounds, but others from loving, stable families.

US psychiatrist Donald Black, author of *Bad Boys, Bad Men*, did an exhaustive study of Dylan Klebold and Eric Harris, the two teenage boys who mowed down twelve fellow students and one teacher at Columbine High School in Colorado in 1999. He concluded they both had anti-social personality disorders attributable to—who knows what. 'It's a myth that behind any horrific act like this there must be some kind of long-time trauma or abuse,' noted Black. 'Most anti-social children I treat have pretty normal parents and pretty ordinary home lives.'

Fifty per cent of serial killers come from a damaged upbringing, which leaves 50 per cent who don't. Far from suffering from poor self-image, studies show that some criminals have a superiority complex, a feeling of entitlement that fuels their aggression when they don't get what they want, whenever they want it. Mix that in with a culture that devalues and dehumanises gay men, so their lives are seen to have less value, and you can see why some young roughs make a hobby of 'poofter bashing' to bolster their own shallow sense of machismo. The persecution that begins in the primary-school playground with teasing and taunts of any boy who is 'different' can all too easily morph into physical abuse or worse once males enter the emotional storms of adolescence.

Some people inevitably rationalise away anti-gay violence with, 'This doesn't affect me: I'm not gay, nor is my son, nor any of my family.' But as long as there remains even a smidgin of sympathy for those who carry out anti-gay crimes, none of us is safe. As we have seen in this book, it's not unusual for heterosexual or married men to be mistaken for being gay—and to be beaten up and killed. For one reason or another, some young males never learn to put a brake on their internal aggression, and when they want to flex their machismo, women and gay men are the easiest targets. As we have seen, gay-bashers are more often than not women bashers as well.

We now live in a society where the average child, by the time they are eighteen, is exposed to 40 000 acts of violence in the general media. Few researchers bother any longer to dispute that bloodshed on television and in the movies, and in hunt-and-kill computer games, leads to increasing desensitisation to violence in real life. Not that a violent film or television show turns a responsible kid into a criminal; what it does do is feed the fertile imagination of a teenager already inclined to be ruthless and aggressive. It is but one piece in the complex puzzle of youth violence.

While we may never know the exact circumstances surrounding the hellish deaths of John Russell and Ross Warren, what has became abundantly clear through Stephen Page's investigation is that a gang of teenage thugs were engaged in a murder spree. They weren't hardened criminals in the strictest sense—or at least, back in 1989 and 1990, they weren't. But like all gangs, from the Los Angeles Crips to the Mafia, they followed a couple of ringleaders and happily did their bidding. Throughout Steve Page's investigation the path kept winding back to three or four main suspects who were involved in gay bashings at Bondi, but there were too many blind spots in the evidence to formally lay charges.

The murderers of John Russell and Ross Warren are free men, getting on with their lives. Do they ever give any thought to the lives they have wiped out, the families they have destroyed, the loved ones and friends still suffering to this day? Do they feel any real remorse, suffer any genuine moral pangs?

Don't count on it. As we have witnessed in ugly close-up through the phone-tapping and listening devices of Operation Taradale, any apparent regrets by the perpetrators tend to be confined to the courtroom *after* they have been caught. A few crocodile tears before the jury, a few remorseful words to the judge, but only until they are back with their mates in a pub or a prison cell, where the ghastly gloating about 'rolling fags' and 'throwing faggots off a cliff' cranks up again.

So where does that leave us? Is there anything our society can do?

'All I can do is urge communities . . . to regard victimisation of a gay man or lesbian as completely abhorrent and not to be tolerated,' declared Coroner Jacqueline Milledge in her final summing up.

Our only real hope of combating gay hatred, of course, is to start in our schools. Just as kids can be taught hatred and intolerance, so they can be taught respect for those different from themselves, to value people equally, and to see prejudice against gays and lesbians as deeply uncool and unacceptable. Religious conservatives inevitably—and predictably—complain that this amounts to promoting homosexuality, but you can no more teach someone to be gay than to be left-handed. The weight of scientific evidence—that

...osexuality is biologically determined—is now ...ported by studies of the animal and insect kingdoms, ...ere homosexual behaviour is surprisingly common ...ross all species.

In any case, if homosexuality *were* a matter of choice rather than predetermined genetic design, does anyone seriously think they would opt for a life of discrimination, harassment and potential victimisation?

After all, the victims in this book lost their lives, not because they were bad, or had robbed a bank, or had struggled with a jealous lover, or had fallen foul of the Mafia.

They died because they were gay.